Testimony

My writings got me into a great deal of trouble. My fellow Greeks were very rational and I was accused of being a mystic and was almost killed. If I had read this book back then I would have saved myself a great deal of aggravation. Do yourself a favor and read this book today.

Plato
Channelled by Trudy Lumphkin
October, 1996

Hal and Sidra are terrible writers. I don't know why they asked me to give a testimonial. I happen to be British and so there aren't many things I like. I haven't written any books myself because I can't stand being criticized. I much prefer being a book critic than the other way around. This is a terrible book and there is no point to it at all.

Waldo Lester
Leicester, England

This book is a milestone in the work of the Drs. Stone. It is difficult to imagine a life full of freedom with an end to self criticism. Everytime I get the impulse to go to my desk and work, I now talk to my husband or pick up one of my cats. I have started to drink coffee again after giving it up in a great cleansing program when I was five years old. This has helped me very much too. My one criticism is that I think the title is terrible. I would have called it: "Embracing Your Non-Writer" or "Embracing Your Procrastinator" or "Embracing" something. So I have decided that whenever I tell one of my friends about the book, I refer to it as "Embracing Your Non-Writer" and now I feel better.

Sally Winbotham
Adelaide, Australia

Dear Hal and Sidra,

I have been a professional woman and a writer all my adult life. I never paid any attention to my environment. It never mattered to me. I just wrote books and articles and paid no attention to my home. Then I came upon the chapter on "Organizing Your Home" in your latest book and suddenly light bulbs started to go off in my head.

Suddenly I found within myself the "Inner Mother" and "Happy Housekeeper" I had lost when I rejected my real mother at the age of three months. My therapist at that time helped me to see that she was the total housewife/mother type and I never could bear being with her. I do think that I was a little young to be given these insights and in hindsight, I do believe that my therapist did have a mother problem.

At any rate, with the help of this wonderful book by you, Hal and Sidra Stone, I have given up writing and my life is filled with the richness of housekeeping and motherhood. I am now ecstatically pregnant and the doctor said it might be triplets. My 3 dogs and 4 cats make it difficult at times to maintain order, but for me it is a full time job. I feel as though I have finally "come home" to my real self and my true calling. Now all I need is a husband but I know that I will meet the right man soon.

Deidra Swallow
Awesome Wells, Arizona

In learning how to be a non-writer I have spent a total of $165,000 over the past year. I bought a large computer and also a lap top computer for myself and then my wife wanted the same. I needed a study for myself in order to have privacy for my writing and so my wife wanted a study for herself. I built two small rooms onto my home. My car was causing me a great deal of irritation with its constant breakdowns so I bought a new one. Needless to say, my wife wanted a new one too. I am working two jobs now and I am exhausted. In addition to spending all this money, I have very high monthly payments. One thing is for sure, who has time to write? Thank you for your help. For my money you could make it less expensive to become a non-writer!

Fermin Rauschen
Hong Kong

This handy how-to handbook has saved me from many a creative outburst! I, too, could have been stuck in the mush of a romantic novel, tied to the gore of an action-packed thriller, or enslaved to the imagined future in a science fiction story if it weren't for this enlightened approach to non-writing. Leave it to Hal and Sidra who are well known for walking their walk and talking their talk. Follow in their non-footsteps to literary relaxation and enjoy the slide! A must to own and non-read!!

Marilou Brewer
Office & Marketing Manager
for Hal and Sidra Stone

You don't <u>have</u> to write a book!

The Procrastination Manual for Aspiring Writers & Doers

By

HAL STONE, PhD and SIDRA STONE, PhD

Other books by Hal and Sidra Stone:
(Oops, these snuck by us…)

The Shadow King, Sidra Stone, PhD
Embracing Heaven and Earth, Hal Stone, PhD
Embracing Our Selves, Drs. Hal & Sidra Stone
Embracing Each Other, Drs. Hal & Sidra Stone
Embracing Your Inner Critic, Drs. Hal & Sidra Stone

Appendix D has a complete list of titles
by Drs. Hal & Sidra Stone

You Don't Have to Write a Book!
Published by Delos, Inc.
© 1997 Hal and Sidra Stone

Cover Design:
Judy Brown

Book layout and design:
Platt & Company

Photographs:
Sidra Stone, Hal Stone, Marilou Brewer, Antonia Lamb

Table of Contents

DEDICATION

This book is dedicated to those forgotten people of the world, the non-doers. More specifically, it is dedicated to those people of the world who thought of writing a book but didn't do it. This is very hard work requiring much skill and perseverance. Those who have learned "how not to" are our heroes and heroines, always forgotten when praise and credit are given for the advancement of civilization. Though we *have* written several books, we consider ourselves successful non-writers because through the years we have thought of writing a multitude of additional books that we have *not* written.

In a sense we are all non-writers and we must learn to appreciate ourselves properly. This book, then, is dedicated to you and to us. Let us sing praise to all of us for our non-writing achievements!

Hal and Sidra Stone
Albion, California
February, 1997

INTRODUCTION

arly in 1933, Hal had a dream. In this dream, an old man with flowing robes, silver hair and a radiant countenance looked upon him and spoke the following words: "Harold, my son," he was known as Harold at that time, "Harold, my son, you come from a long and a noble lineage and you have an important gift to bring to the world when you become a man. There will come a time at the end of this century when the world will be inundated with 'how to' books telling people how to grow and how to do more with their lives. People will feel pushed to produce more and more. Each will feel the need to write a book, an important book. It will be necessary for someone to 'Protect People from this Push toward Prolific Production.' You have been assigned this task, this mission. It will be difficult, some say it will be an impossible mission." Young Harold, already creative, thought: "Mission impossible, that sounds good."

Hal, although only six years old at that time, knew that this was an important dream. He couldn't wait until the next morning to tell it to his mother. When he woke her at 3 AM to share his excitement with her, she told him he must have eaten too much cotton candy and that he should go back to sleep. He did so and promptly forgot his dream.

Many years later Hal and I were watching Mission Impossible and I was gently snoring. (I'm not sure why it is, but all my husbands seem to love Mission Impossible and it's always put me to sleep.) Suddenly, Hal arose from his chair and, smiling an enigmatic smile, turned off the TV and began to move gracefully towards his computer. His movements and an unusual radiance that surrounded him roused me from my slumber. I asked him what made him glow like that and why he wasn't watching his TV program. He said, "The dream, the dream, I just remembered my dream.

It is time for me to fulfill the prophetic words of the wise old man, it is time for me to carry out my mission!" So it was that Hal began to write this book and I have done all that I could to help him.
Sidra Stone

We are proud to present to you the first "how not to" book. Our aim is to elevate the creative process of non-achievement (with non-writing as our metaphor) as a legitimate path to consciousness. This will give it a proper place in the history of psychology, consciousness and the transformational journey!

This book is a compendium of wisdom, a veritable encyclopedia of procrastination. Over the past 20 years we have had many different ideas about books that we wished to write. There are so many of them that we cannot possibly remember them all, although we do have files full of book outlines.

The number of these unwritten books, were we to count them, could easily reach into the hundreds, possibly even the thousands. This has always been a source of pain and existential angst for each of us. But, since the dream **was** recalled, our lives have changed. NO MORE! NO MORE! NO MORE! No more apologies! No more excuses! We now realize that our non-writing was the fulfilling of a prophecy. We are proud now of the amazing versatility we displayed in these years of creative procrastination. Now our only desire is to share this treasure with you, our dear readers.

As we have said, we are not just talking about non-writing; the larger issue is non-doing. Although this theoretical and methodological system concentrates upon non-writing, we want you to understand that you can extend this information and use these techniques to deal with all of your "required" activities. Your days of guilt about what you have *not* accomplished are over once you read and apply the principles of this book.

We apologize to you for writing a book to teach you the joys of non-writing. We simply could not think of any better way to convey this information. When you consider all the books that we did *not* write, we hope that you can forgive us for bringing this one into the world. Good luck to you in all your non-writing endeavors, and may we all find honor and companionship on "the path of non-writing" described in the pages that follow.

Hal and Sidra Stone
Albion, California
February, 1997

Section I

Preparing To Write:
How To Postpone
The Start Of Writing

Hal Talking About Book

Here is Hal talking about a book he is thinking about writing. Remember the basic principle! If you talk long enough about something you have a good chance of killing it. From the involvement of Hal and his audience, it would appear that he has a good chance of non-writing success.

1

Talking
About the Book

Non-writing does not have to be a downer. As we thought about the many books we hadn't written (whether individually or jointly), we realized how enormously creative we have been in our procrastination! You, our dear reader, can be as successful as we have been. You will be able to enjoy this feeling of creativity and well-being and to breathe in the light that comes with the acceptance of your non-writing nature.

L earning the art of non-writing begins the very first moment you have a thought about writing a book. If you bypass this first step, you will miss one of your greatest opportunities of becoming a non-writer. Simply put, this first step is as follows: Share each of your ideas as it emerges! This is a technique that has been used effectively by non-writers since its first discovery by Tom E. Addison. He found that there is only a certain amount of energy in the universe for each book and this energy cannot be created, destroyed or changed. Thus, if you talk about your book instead of writing it, you will use up its allotment of energy in talking and you will never have to write it. Voila! You have become a non-writer with minimal effort.

We know many people who have needed no more than this first bit of guidance to become successful non-writers. They are very popular at literary cocktail parties because they always have wonderfully creative new book ideas to discuss. Hostesses love them because they keep the other guests entertained for hours. Admittedly, this is a relatively superficial sharing with people that they don't know very well, but the numbers are advantageous. The most successful of these non-writers have been known to share book ideas with dozens of people an evening, thereby dissipating the book energy quickly and efficiently.

If you are not interested in these more scientific considerations, i.e., the dissipation of energy, you can focus upon another aspect of this sharing. Think of it as spreading your ideas around rather than keeping them selfishly to yourself. This will allow you to experience a largesse of spirit about sharing your ideas with family, intimate friends, casual relationships, people at work and anyone else who will listen. The more that you talk about your forthcoming book, the better off you are in your movement towards becoming a non-writer.

In addition to the aura of abundance that will surround you as you share your many ideas, you will be proving to others that you are not a private person who holds secrets from them. People don't like it when we keep secrets from them! Imagine what would happen if you wrote a book and no one knew that you were writing it. Suddenly your book is released and there it is, piled up in tall stacks in all of your local bookstores. Imagine how your family, your friends, and even your acquaintances would feel. They would feel hurt and left out. Every one of them would be angry with you. You don't want to risk the displeasure of so many people. Certainly this alone should provide you with a high motivation for sharing.

There is one more reason for sharing your book ideas as soon as they emerge: You need feedback from as many people as possible so that you know how people will react to your book once it is written. This will save you pain and embarrassment later when everything is in print and you can no longer change your mind. You will have eager responses to your request for feedback. People simply love to express their feelings, ideas and reactions. You can occupy many a fruitful hour listening to what they have to say about your plans. They will have many suggestions. You can record these and then consider them as you work on your outline. It is true that all these suggestions about your book are very likely to confuse you, but this entire process will aid you tremendously in your attempts to postpone the moment when you actually sit down and begin to write.

Do not limit this sharing to your close relationships, even though you may have many friends with an abundance of ideas. What you want is serious feedback. Intimate friends may encourage you and leave it at that. People with whom you have more distant relationships may respond very differently to your ideas, so you want to be sure that you spread your new ideas around as much as possible and check them out with all sorts of people.

If your parents are living, tell them what you are thinking about. Try it. Don't assume they won't understand. Let your brothers and sisters know that you are ready to write a book. They may not give you feedback directly, but if you "tune into your gut reactions," you will have a sense of what they are thinking or feeling.

It is entirely possible that you will feel some negativity from some people about what you are proposing. Siblings, in particular, may not appreciate your creative efforts. Just always keep in mind this axiom for non-writing: "Negativity is good." The worse the feedback makes you feel, the stronger the possibility that non-writing will win out over writing. Thus you will be freed of the burden of writing and as a result you will have time to play or to do whatever you really want to do.

We have heard it said that it is possible to talk a thing to death. Well, if you talk about your proposed book often enough, long enough, and with a sufficient number of people, you can do just that! If so, we would have to consider this a very successful conclusion to our first chapter.

If you are fortunate enough to join the ranks of those who became non-writers after reading just this first chapter, then it is not necessary to read the remainder of the book. You might think about passing it on to others who have been bitten by the writing bug or else setting it aside in case the writing bug bites you again, which it well may do.

Exercises

For this exercise we would like you to use a project that you have been daydreaming about. It might be a book, or it might be some other creative project that interests you. Talk to ten people about your idea and then answer the following questions for yourself?

1. How did you feel talking to the different people?

2. Was the feedback valuable for your project?

3. Was there anyone that you felt like punching in the nose?

4. Do you feel like continuing the project now?

5. Would it have felt better if you had talked to twenty people?

This exercise should help you to determine the value of talking to people as a vehicle for non-writing. Because we are all different, each of us must discover which non-writing techniques work most effectively for our particular needs. If you have not yet postponed your plans for writing indefinitely, read on. You may find that some ideas in later chapters will work better for you.

2

Being Special:
Rejecting Ordinary

The more special you want your book to be,
the less chance there is that it will ever be written.
Ancient Wisdom

A s a new author you certainly do not want to be ordinary! Ordinary is bad! Just think of the hundreds and thousands of books written each year. You don't want to be just one of the herd! You want to be the leader! The winner! The home run hitter! We will now reveal to you one of the best-kept secrets of the ancient sages: "The more special you want your book to be, the less chance there is that it will ever be written."

It can take a great deal of time to be sure that the book you are about to write is special. We suggest that you repeat the exercises suggested in Chapter 1 in order to evaluate your ideas with others again and again. In this way you can be reassured that your forthcoming book will be different from, and better than, all the others. You don't want to risk putting anything out there that is not guaranteed special. If there is any indication that your book might be just ordinary, scrap your idea and start over.

By now you can see that it is extremely important for your development as a non-writer that you see yourself as a very special person. You must eschew anything that might suggest you are ordinary. We recommend an ongoing mantra or affirmation in which you would say either silently or out loud: "I AM

SPECIAL! I AM SPECIAL! I am special in every way! In every way I am special! Every day in every way I am becoming more and more special." These are but a few of the possibilities. Use your creativity to think of a truly special mantra of your very own.

In general, our society is one that worships specialness and abhors ordinariness. If you ask the average person how he or she feels about the idea of being ordinary, the reaction you get is generally unfavorable. People hate being ordinary. This is very much in your favor because there is constant support from your surroundings for all your efforts to get rid of your "ordinariness."

If you pay attention you will see the ways in which our society is oriented towards "being special". Our movies and television promote specialness. Our advertising shows us models who are very, very special. Have you ever seen an ordinary kiss in a movie, or an ordinary looking model in a magazine? Is anyone ever permitted to have an ordinary time any more, or must we all be joyous and excited about everything from our toothpaste to our beer? The advertisements we watch on television show us very special food, very special drinks, very special cars, and very special men and women in very special clothing. Even our dogs and cats are very special as they eat their very special food out of very special dishes.

It is true that sometimes the drive to be special has actually pushed someone into *writing* a book. Usually, however, it tends to work in just the opposite way and the drive for specialness works against writing. This is why it is so valuable for us in our work. It tends to create grandiose ideas and plans that make us feel as though we needed to climb Mt. Everest rather than take a pleasant stroll down the road. We shall see in later chapters how this quality of being special operates in different phases of book writing.

To summarize then, if you wish to become a successful non-writer, you must avoid being ordinary. If it was all right to be ordinary, then you might simply sit down and write a book without worrying about how good or special it was. You might even focus on the ideas instead of on how the book would be received by the world and how special it would make you feel. We hope that you now understand why it is essential to focus upon how to be special and that you further realize that feeling ordinary is dangerous. It can result in effortless and pleasant writing. You might even *enjoy* writing a book and this could conceivably destroy your chances of becoming a non-writer forever.

3

Planning to Write
More Than One Book

Feeling special about yourself helps to create a sense of omnipotence about your abilities and your physical stamina. You can do anything, so the more books planned, the better.

Why write only one book at a time? Anyone can write one book, but it takes somebody really special to write more than one book at the same time. If not several books simultaneously, then how about a *series* of books instead of just the one you were planning to write in the first place?

This plan goes along with the idea of being special. After all, two books are better than one and four books are certainly better than two. Feeling special about yourself helps to create a sense of omnipotence about your abilities and your physical stamina. You can do anything if you are truly special, so the more books planned, the better.

There are two ways to approach the idea of multiple books. The first way is to write more than one book at a time. In this modern day of computers, all this requires is that you open a new folder on your hard disc and give it a name. In less than a minute you are writing an additional book. It is really that simple and it feels simply marvelous. In our life experience there are few peak experiences as exhilarating as looking in your computer and seeing four or five or even six new folders listing books that you are planning to write.

We recall reading about a very prolific American author, Jamie Misher, who has three or four books going at any one time, each on a different topic. In a recent interview, she said that it kept her daily writing schedule more interesting. If **she** can do it, certainly **you** can do it. As a matter of fact, at this very moment Hal has four folders on his hard drive, each with the name of a prospective book on it. Actually, Hal has little or nothing in his folders, but this doesn't matter. There they are, waiting to be filled, constant reminders of the writing that needs to be done. A procrastinator's paradise!

The second way to approach this issue of writing more than one book, and probably the more common, is to plan to write a series of books. In this way you start planning, even outlining, the whole series. This can occupy considerable time. Your original book now is part of a greater whole. You may even be outlining a lifetime endeavor. In this way you have the sense of a writing process that is timeless in scope. At this point we suggest that you review the principles of Chapter 1 and proceed to tell people about your new, expanded plans to write a series of books. Follow up with the principles of Chapter 2, and let people know how special you are.

It is true that you may face some embarrassment if you never write anything, but think of all the free time you will have once you are no longer writing, time to do the things that you really want to do. Jawahl Singh, a recovering writer, has this to say about the multiple book recommendations that we have made in this chapter.

Dear Dr. Stone and Dr. Stone,

For over ten years I was a successful writer. Then I came across the ideas of non-writing proposed by the two of you in

*an article published originally in a local consciousness maga-
zine. I was especially struck by your remarkable recommendations about planning a book series. Prior to this I had written
over a dozen books, both fiction and non-fiction. I knew that
something was wrong but I couldn't put my finger on exactly
what it was.*

*Immediately after reading your article, I planned a 12 book
series that was designed to deal with the religious history, philosophy and psychology of Indian thinkers since 5,000 BC.
My dear friends, that was absolutely and without doubt the
breakthrough of my life and, I am happy to say, the end of my
writing career.*

*Now I enjoy myself to pieces doing something that I have
always wanted to do but my father never permitted in our
family. I am racing sports cars for the Bombay/Calcutta Racing Association. Thank you so very much for your ideas and
especially for the deeply compassionate and non-judgmental
way that you talk about these issues.*

Please feel free to use this letter as you wish.

Jawahl Singh
Bombay, India

We cite this quote from Mr. Singh to illustrate the full power
and majesty of the multiple or serial book plan. We very much
encourage you to put this plan into effect immediately. We ourselves are so excited by the idea that we are considering writing
a series of books on non-writing that would include full workbooks. This has led Hal to also consider a book series on: "How
to Stop Drinking Coffee." He is well suited to this task since he
has stopped drinking coffee almost as often as he has not written a book that he wanted to write.

Sidra With Cover Artist

It is very important to have an outstanding artist who can prepare the cover of a book. Here is Sidra with Judy Brown, cover artist for her Patriarch Book (The Shadow King). Judy, naturally enough, is trying to convince us to write other books so she can make more covers for us. Sidra is very lovingly attempting to explain to her the principles of non-writing and it does appear from this picture that Judy is finally beginning to understand the theory.

4

Finding
the Right Title

What you must always keep in mind is the fundamental tenet of our cutting edge non-writing theory: "Anything that causes a delay is good."

Finding the right title and sub-title for your book is a grand adventure and you cannot start it soon enough. A good title sells books and creates a focus for the writer so you must plan to spend ample time choosing your title. We want to assist you in this process because it can be an extremely effective way of delaying the actual writing of your book. There are several basic principles to be considered regarding the development of your book title.

First Principle: Under no circumstances should you attempt to start writing until you have a proper title in mind. Tell yourself that you can waste an extraordinary amount of time writing if you begin to write before you have the clarity that will be provided by your book title. After all, how can you write if you don't know what you are writing about?

Second Principle: The sub-title is just as important as the title and it is essential that this, too, be clearly set before the onset of any actual writing. The keyword here is "FOCUS". You must have a clear focus before you start to write. Otherwise your thoughts will be blurry and not focused and you may even ramble. Even if you enjoy this kind of writing, do not let your-self be seduced. Get that title and subtitle first.

Third Principle: For successful non-writing, you must not trust your basic intuition about the title. Please note that choosing a title is again a time for sharing, for talking with as many people as possible. Think about having a gathering at your home or apartment and allowing everyone to give input into the process of name selection. After all, is finding a name for a book any less important than finding a name for a new baby? Not at all! A baby can always change his or her name at a later age. A book's title is forever. Choosing it deserves our full attention.

Fourth Principle: Take advantage of different language dictionaries and lexicons. You have no idea where you might discover just the right name and these are good places to look. You can also do a literature search and find out what kinds of titles have been used in your particular subject area. With the new computer that you are going to own (See Chapter 6), you can utilize many new high-tech sources of information to aid you in your title research. If you like a more simple and earthy approach, you can walk through libraries and bookstores and study the different titles you see there.

Fifth Principle: The key to finding a good title is research. The more time that you take finding just the right title, the better off you will be in the long run. Once you have chosen your title, it is necessary to develop a good subtitle. The same procedures can be effective here that we have described in finding the main title. Remember to secure as much input as you can and stay away from your own intuitions which can lead you down a false trail and bring much embarrassment. It is also possible that your own intuitions might provide you with an appropriate title immediately and you would lose an excellent source of procrastination.

Sixth Principle: Part of the excitement of a new title is the way it will look on the front of the book. While you are working to discover a good name for your book, you can begin to visualize how you would like the book to look. Do you want a picture of yourself on the front cover, the back cover, or on the inside flap? What colors would you like? While you are researching a title in the libraries and bookstores, take some extra time to study the front and back covers of the books to see which ones you like best.

The combination of searching for the perfect title and subtitle for your book and developing your own aesthetic sense of book cover design could well take several months of intensive self-discipline and research. These months of investigation are all good solid non-writing months and will help you to postpone the beginning of your book. What you must always keep in mind is the fundamental tenet of our cutting edge non-writing theory: "Anything that causes a delay is good."

5

Choosing the Right Publisher/Agent

Ordinarily one would think that it is appropriate to start your book before looking for an agent or publisher. Not so!

I t is never too early in the book writing process to find an agent and/or a publisher. Before you even begin to write, it is a good idea to think about whether you want to use an agent for your book or whether you want to deal with the publishers on your own. In either case, the key to the problem is research. There is a great deal of investigation required in order to come up with the best answer for you, your book and your own special requirements.

There are then three basic principles that you need to keep in mind when thinking about a publisher/agent:

First Principle: Start your planning and research the moment that you have the idea of writing your book.

Second Principle: Research the publishing world thoroughly by contacting all the agents that you can find and all the publishing companies that you can find.

Third Principle: Wherever possible, arrange for personal interviews with everyone on your list, even those who live in other cities.

Ordinarily one would think that it is appropriate to start your book before looking for an agent or publisher. Not so! There is something very satisfying about exploring the world of publishing. You start out a virgin and after many months you still feel like a virgin, though a bit shopworn. Talking to agents and publishers is the way to become a pro. Wouldn't it be nice, now that you have an idea for a book, to already have an agent/publisher locked up? Wouldn't that make you feel more sure of yourself when it comes to the actual writing?

You have no idea how many agents there are. You have even less of an idea how many publishers there are, that is, unless you have already published a book. Incidentally, we have no fear of suggesting these activities to well-established authors who have already been published. We have helped many of them to terminate their status as writers by recommending that they spend more time with publishers and agents. Publishers and agents often have a way with words that tends to depress aspiring writers and turn them into non-writers which is, of course, what this book is about.

Once you get the names of the different agents, you will want to meet with them. They may want to see a book or a part of a book. Don't let that put you off. Meet them first. Insist on a conference so that you can see whether or not your personalities mesh. The worst thing in the world is to work with an agent whose personality doesn't mesh with yours. Don't be seduced by an agent's guarantee of an advance of $100,000. Make sure the vibes are right. Is a published book worth the lack of harmony you may experience in such a situation? Is the money worth the price of the discomfort? Of course not! So make sure of the fit!

Now that you have spent weeks, or even months, interviewing agents, you are ready to move on to publishers. There are hundreds of publishing houses. Either buy the source books that list the names and addresses of these companies or see about finding this information via computer. This is guaranteed to provide you with an overwhelming amount of time-consuming information. You will find big publishing houses and small ones. There are even combinations of large and small in the form of small publishing groups that are a part of larger companies. Some companies specialize in particular subjects. Last but not least, there are publishing houses that will enable you to publish your own book and keep the ultimate control over what happens to it.

Next, go to the book store and look at all the new books that have come out during the past couple of months. Touch them, open them. Look at the cover art, the cover text, the way in which the book itself is typeset. Which publishing company produces the most attractive books? Which company's books seem most compatible with your way of thinking? When you have the answers to these questions, you can begin to contact these publishing houses on an individual basis. Wherever possible, arrange an interview with someone in the company. The more interviews the better.

There are things to look for when you are interviewing publishing companies and agents:

1. You must find someone who is comfortable with our ideas about non-writing so that when you don't finish your book the publisher will not be too upset.

2. You must find a publishing company willing to accept blame if your book doesn't sell. Otherwise, if your book doesn't sell, you must face the fact that it isn't very interesting. This is really a terrible alternative!

3. You must search until you find a publishing company that believes in giving large advances on books promised but not yet written. No matter how long it takes to find such a company, keep looking. They are out there...somewhere.

4. You must look for a publisher who will guarantee a fully funded 20 city tour for book promotion. You can compromise at 16 cities. You want to get the message out there and these tours are a very important way to make contact with a large number of people and bookstores.

5. You must find a publisher who will guarantee you that a full time Publicist will be assigned to your book. Publishers tend to be very good about this sort of thing.

6. You must find a publisher who will invest in training you to present your work to the media. It is never too early to begin working with someone who can help you prepare for your coming book tour.

Some of these guidelines sound fairly rigorous. We realize this and we also realize that much of this research may seem like dull work, but non-writing is a serious undertaking and we are not here to coddle you. Just keep in mind the ultimate purpose of the painstaking research that we suggest in this book. It is worth all the effort we are recommending.

Sidra at Computer in Spider Web

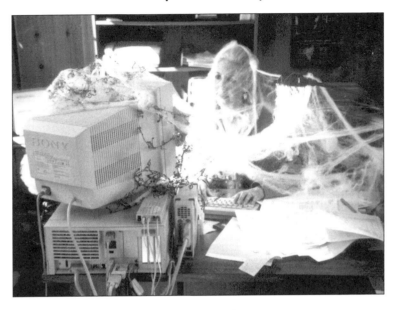

Becoming an expert in using your new computer is an essential requirement for every writer. Here is Sidra who has become so lost in her self training program that spider webs have grown all around her. This dedication will pay off once she has mastered all of the intricacies of her computer and she is able finally to apply her efforts to her long delayed book.

6

Purchasing
a New Computer

The moment you have the idea of writing a book, begin to plan for the purchase of your new computer. Don't waste a moment deciding whether or not this is a good idea. This is a marvelous idea so just go out and do it!

You cannot possibly start writing a new book without a new computer. God would strike you dead. It doesn't matter whether you have written a book before or this is your first book. A new computer is an absolute must! Give up any idea of writing a book with a pen, typing it on a typewriter, writing with a pencil and eraser on a big yellow pad, or using the same computer that you have used in recent years. You might as well think of using a well-sharpened goose quill and an inkwell. The new technology makes writing an excitement that you simply cannot miss. The new computers can do everything but make love to you and almost anything is possible in the next generation.

Your new computer will be special and will make you special (See Chapter 2). It can do an unlimited number of *special* things. It will undoubtedly speed up the writing process once you have purchased it, set it up, and learned how to use it. In this chapter we will focus on the first of these matters, the purchase. There are a number of steps involved in buying a new computer:

Buying Your New Computer

1. The moment you have the idea of writing a book, begin to plan for the purchase of your new computer. Don't waste a moment deciding whether or not this is a good idea. It is, so just go out and do it. Everyone knows that your new computer will just about write the book for you.

2. Talk to as many people as you can about which computer they think is the best for your needs. Here you will come up against a major decision that will probably affect the course of your life. Are you a Macintosh® type or an IBM® type? It is a fact today that the vast majority of computers sold are IBM® clones or others based on the use of the Pentium® chip. Nevertheless, the Mac® followers make up for their lower sales figures by virtue of their enthusiasm, some might even say fanatical loyalty to their product.

   It is quite likely that you do not think of yourself as a type at all. You may, in fact, be very unhappy with the notion of being typed in any way or on any level in your life. However, once you make this decision, whatever *your* intent may be, you will fall into either the Mac® or IBM® category.

   To our knowledge there are currently no formal psychological profiles or official testing procedures that have been developed to describe Mac® and IBM® people. Thus there are no objective measures to help you in making your decision. However, on an informal level, there seems to be a general agreement that the major difference between the groups is: (a) Mac® people like to talk about how much fun it is to use the system; (b)

IBM® people feel that the work they do is very, very serious and they need a very serious computer to handle it; (c) There seems to be a preponderance of Mac® users on the west coast.

We don't at all mean to imply that computers have real personalities, but, then again, maybe they do. Or maybe it is all projection. Whatever the case, many people say that the Macintosh® has a warmer and a friendlier personality than the IBM® (or PC as they are sometimes called). This may have something to do with the friendly smiling face and little beep that greets you each time you turn on your Macintosh.® IBM® people will say that the Macintosh is more of a powder puff, not meant for truly serious work. Some people think that the IBM® users are Eastern Establishment types and Mac® users are more the Western or California type. Which type are you?

Though the judgments do fly between the two camps, we can assure you that an owner of an IBM® system computer can live in harmony with the owner of a Macintosh® computer as long as they deal with the underlying judgments and conflicts that necessarily accompany this unfortunate state of affairs.

On a purely personal note, we have found that although we have Macs and the majority of our children have IBM® clones, we have been able to work out a way to be civil about our differences. However, sometimes counseling or mediation is necessary for mixed households when the parties themselves cannot deal effectively with their differences. Most important of all, you must be aware that it is possible to be a successful non-writer with *either* system.

3. There are a vast number of computer stores and your next task, after having talked to friends and acquaintances, is to visit the professionals. Go to the stores and try out the machines. Talk to the sales people and the service people and get the real poop about each one. We promise that this will be a great deal of fun and, if approached systematically, can occupy a considerable amount of time. Take notes.

When you are satisfied that you have left no stone unturned, go home and review these notes with the friends and family members who have given you advice already. Everyone will be happy to help you to think about this decision. You will note that there are a lot of computer experts around. Please keep in mind the fact that the more complex and technical your computer, the longer it will take you to figure out how to use it, and the more glitches you are likely to encounter. We promise that this will keep you very busy and give you a simply grand opportunity to postpone your writing.

4. Now on to other decisions! You might think that deciding upon a computer completes this process and that you can now proceed with your writing. But, no, there is more, much more. If this is your first foray into the world of computers, you will undoubtedly be as surprised as we were to discover that once you have chosen your computer, you have a number of other decisions to make about your system. What kind of monitor do you want? You can have 14, 15, or 17 inches... or even larger. Do you want color? Of course you want color! For the potential non-writer aesthetics are very important and aesthetics without color are difficult to imagine. You can have great fun with color, too, even though you don't need it to write a book.

You can get CD ROM which is really exciting even though it might not be germane to your book project. Everyone has CD ROM these days and it doesn't feel very good to be left out of the fun. Our own perspective is that even though you may never use it, it is better to have it. One never knows when there may be a bit of research that is only available on a CD ROM. Feeling a sense of inadequacy is not going to support what you are trying to do in life and most certainly you will be filled with feelings of inadequacy if you don't have a CD ROM capability and others do.

Next there is the fax modem. As a writer you must have a fax modem so that you can communicate with other writers. You can use it to send your material directly to your editor as soon as you write it. (Actually, if you become a successful *non*-writer, you will never have anything to send to anyone. But that is neither here nor there!) It is a good feeling to think of being able to send out your material directly from your computer. Then your editor can edit it and send it back. A writer who is special and who is going to write a special book or a special book series with a very special title and a special publishing company ought properly to have all the special things that go along with a very special computer. Don't you agree?

The last thing you must consider is your printer. You can of course get either a black and white or a color printer. Some people like to have both. Once again it is a question of taking the time that is necessary to research the field and see what best meets your needs even though, hopefully, you may never use it for a book.

When all is said and done, the best thing is to get everything and anything that you can buy for your computer. The research you do will undoubtedly lead you to this inevitable decision.

5. No, you are not yet finished with decision making. You also must decide whether to purchase a small portable model or a larger desk size model. As a serious writer you might want to have both. With a portable model you have the freedom to have the computer with you at all times. You can never tell when inspiration might strike you and you certainly don't want to be caught without a computer at the crucial moment. On the other hand, when you are at your desk, wouldn't it be more comfortable to work with a larger keyboard and screen? There are also the small portables that dock into a larger system. These last either simplify your decision or add to its complexity, depending on how you look at things. So many questions, so many possible answers! It is the process of search and research that matters, so enjoy all of this pre-writing activity. It can keep you busy for a very, very long time.

    We have one last point to make, now that you come this far. As you make these decisions regarding your computer purchase, keep in mind that the more you spend, the less you have in the bank. The less you have in the bank, the more hours you must work to earn money. So, the fundamental principle here is to overspend so that you feel the need to work harder on your regular job. You might not ordinarily think about this aspect of your computer purchase, but it can definitely provide the additional delay you need to successfully postpone the moment you actually sit down and start writing. Believe us when we tell you that maintaining the status of a non-writer requires never-ending vigilance!

Once you have dealt with these basic points and have purchased your new computer (or computers), it is time to learn how to use it (or them). In the next chapter we will give you some priceless pointers on gaining computer mastery. First, however, take some time to complete the following exercises. They will help to guide you in implementing some of the ideas we have presented in this chapter.

Exercises

1. Look in your phone book and see how many stores you can find that sell and service computers. Then call up ten of these stores and get information about their computers. How much are they? What does the salesman recommend, the Mac® or IBM® model? What kind of screen? Should you get CD ROM? Should you get a fax modem? If so, should it be built in or an add on?

2. Visit five computer stores and try out all of their different systems. Keep in mind that your goal is systematic research so don't be afraid to ask questions.

3. Close your eyes and visualize yourself writing your book with a pencil whose point is constantly breaking. After you visualize this, shift your imagery and visualize yourself sitting at your desk typing away on your new computer. Spend a half hour on each visualization for a week in a row. Which one feels better to you?

4. Center yourself in your body. Breathe deeply. Now picture yourself writing down your dreams in the morning with a pencil or pen. Now picture yourself writing down your dreams using a new computer. Which works best for you? We know the answer. Do you?

Sidra With Our Computer Teacher

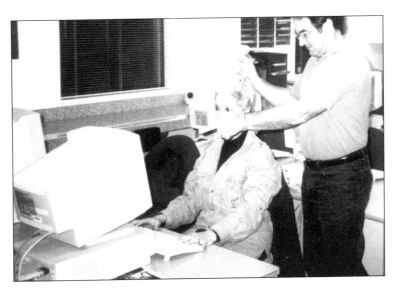

Learning how to use the computer can take years of time. Rennie Innis is in charge of our training program in Mendocino. In this photo, Sidra has been trying to talk about our non-writing book and the principles involved. It is clear that Rennie is not appreciating our non-writing theories. After all, if everyone decided not to write the books they were thinking about writing, then the computer selling business, as well as computer training, would greatly decrease. Here is Rennie attempting to help move Sidra towards silence so he can train her in the use of the internet and other esoteric computer lore.

7

Learning to Use Your New Computer

Do not, under any circumstance, settle for simply learning the word processing program. This is the cowardly way to do things. Take the time necessary to learn everything so you can feel like one of the "big boys"! Even if you don't reach "big boy" status in this lifetime, you can carry your learning into your next incarnation!

Once you have purchased your new computer it is necessary that you learn how to use it. Believe us when we tell you that this can, and should, take a considerable amount of time, particularly if you want to develop mastery rather than just learn the basics of word processing. The key words here are "computer mastery!" Don't settle for anything less.

You will no doubt want to purchase a subscription to one or more computer magazines. If you read these regularly you will be able to keep abreast of the latest software, new product development, and the latest happenings in the computer world. You have a choice in this age of technology. You can become a victim to your new hi-tech equipment and just learn the minimal amount necessary in order to write, fearfully ignoring its vast capabilities. Or you can make up your mind that you are not going to be a victim and that you are going to develop total mastery of its functions. At this juncture we would like to warn you that your new computer has many different functions, not the least of which is the ability to seduce you away from writing forever.

As you read your magazines, you will no doubt see articles about why other systems are better than yours and how your system is already outdated. By constantly updating your equipment, you can balance out the improvements in the new systems and thus make sure that you aren't left behind in the technological frenzy that is sweeping the computer world. You don't want to feel left out or "less than" when you think about others and their equipment. You don't want to suffer from "computer envy" a debilitating psychological disorder described in scholarly detail by Anna Floyd in the very last article she wrote. (Note: After writing that article Anna read our book and stopped writing forever. See Chapter 21)

To get back to your updated computer, you have another choice to make here. Do you wish to take a class and study computer lore in a systematic way? Do you want to hire someone to come to your home and help you there? Do you want to invite a friend to dinner and then sneak up on him or her with your questions? Do you want to go through the manual yourself, alone, and call the 800 numbers for help when you get stuck? Do you want to risk your primary relationship and keep asking your partner how to do things?

Do not, under any circumstance, settle for simply learning the word processing program. As we have said, this is the cowardly way to do things. Take the time necessary to learn everything! You might even consider learning desktop publishing. After all, since you have plans to write a book, what is more natural than learning how to print it yourself and do your own publishing?

There is a vast array of creative uses for your new computer skills. Possibly you could format a newsletter and send it to friends and family a few times a year so they could keep up with your personal and professional activities. If your computer has sound and color, take the time you need to experiment with these. You will want to customize your workspace and get the sounds and colors just right so that the environment they create supports your writing efforts. Some procrastination experts change these sounds and colors daily, much as they change their clothes. A note here to our women readers: You just might want to coordinate your desktop with your outfits each morning.

Then there is the whole world of CD ROM waiting for you. Have you considered the idea of putting your book into a CD ROM format and thus utilizing all the latest interactive word and film technology to express what you want to say? That would truly be cutting edge! This requires time, research and experimentation but the time invested certainly can lead to enormous rewards. There are classes that teach you how to do this.

Now that you have learned how to use your new computer, you have the opportunity of networking into a number of different information systems. These systems require a modem so that you can connect into them and the choices are varied. You can join Internet directly, or you can access the Internet through a number of other organizations such as AOL, CompuServe, various software companies and even many telephone companies. One cannot even begin to think about writing a book today without being a part of this amazing revolution in information gathering.

When you decide to join one of these networks, you must buy the proper software and install it. We personally know of a number of people whose computers went out of commission during this installation process. It took days to straighten things out before they were operable again. Another successful delay, another step towards the ultimate goal of non-writing.

Once installed, these systems are simply smashing. Once you enter any of them, it can easily take hours to exit. There's so much to do and so many people to talk to! Each system is different but they all allow you to send messages anywhere in the world via electronic mail (Email). There is a seemingly endless array of information and communications networks. There are places to go to talk or to listen. There is a new language to learn and new ways of expressing emotions like ":)" (smiley face).

You'll be pleased to note that there is a considerable amount to learn before you can navigate within any of these systems. It is well worth the time it takes, however, when you consider the new world of information and research that becomes available to you. This world is so exciting that many aspiring writers have been known to give up writing entirely and disappear into the net. Their publishers find them years later, still surfing the Internet and gathering the information that will serve them well when they return to their book-to-be. (Many spouses have gotten lost in this way as well. But that is not germane to this particular topic.)

We have many readers who were potential writers but opened their hearts to the inner workings of the various on-line information systems instead of opening their manuscripts. They now lead happy lives deepening their knowledge and experience of computer technology. The following letter is just one among tens of thousands that we have received from individuals who came into contact with our ideas:

Dear Sidra and Hal,

Before I read your book I was writing screen plays and novels, thinking that I was a very successful writer simply because I was earning $750,000 a year. Then I read the first edition of your book and I bought a new computer. That was two years ago. Since that time I have been fully engrossed in learning everything there is to know about computers. I learned desktop publishing as you recommended, though it is true that I have nothing to desktop publish anymore. I have immersed myself in the Internet and continue to be amazed at its possi-

bilities. I belong to two dozen bulletin boards and log in daily. I love it all.

To earn money I have entered a totally new field of work. I got the idea from your chapter on buying computers. I have established a new business as a consultant in conflict resolution. I work with families who are experiencing serious conflict regarding the relative merits of their IBM® or IBM® compatible system and their Mac® counterpart. You can't imagine how much these unresolved issues destroy family harmony. I am swamped with work and though I don't make quite as much, I am very, very happy. Thank you for your ideas and insight.

Norbert Kingsley
President
IBM®-MAC® Consulting Associates
Framingham, MA

As you can clearly see, there are many, many choices that need to be made as you consider training in computer literacy. You will note that the results are well worth the effort.

We have come to the end of the first section of our "how not to" book. It is our hope that the application of the principles found in Chapters 1-7, has either aborted the writing of your book completely, or at least delayed it to a considerable extent.

If you have not stopped writing completely, please move on to Section II. This next section deals with the effective promotion of non-writing through the ongoing organization and re-organization of your personal and professional environments. If your writing has been successfully discontinued, you might want to consider loaning this book to a friend. We don't recommend giving it away because, as we said earlier, you might well need it again in the future if you begin another writing project.

Section II

Organizing Your Environment Before You Write

How to Create Organizational Overload So That You Don't Have Time to Write

Hal Hanging Curtains

Here is Hal doing his share in fixing up the kitchen. There is nothing like freshly laundered curtains to provide a feeling of well-being as one prepares to write......and there is so much to clean.

8

Organizing
Your Home

It is amazing to see what happens when you sit down to write a book. Everything imaginable that needs doing, might need doing or could conceivably need doing far into the distant future comes to your attention.

There is something about the writing process that calls forth the nesting instincts in each of us. Every bird needs to build a nest in which to lay her eggs. Are we any less than the birds? Certainly not. That is why, as soon as you begin to think about writing, you will feel a need to create the proper space for the new life that is germinating within you. The proper space, of course, starts with your home and it is the organization of your home that we will address in this chapter.

You must see that your living space is not only a cozy nest, but it is a *neat*, cozy nest. Everything must be in its proper place because external order is an important part of the creative process. The use of words brings forth a sense of mystery and magic. You have ideas, feelings, fantasies, musings, and opinions and they all want to leap out into the world helter-skelter. Without the creation of order in your environment, there would be chaos in your writing. So it is that you must see that your living space is in proper order. There is a third aspect of this household reorganization to consider – it can be addressed by the ancient art of feng shuey. The energies must flow properly in your home or they will not flow properly in your book.

You may not be the kind of person who ever paid attention to nesting or to order and structure before. You may never have even heard of feng shuey. Now that you are considering a book, this is something that can be put off no longer. You must not procrastinate about organizing your home environment if you wish to be a successful procrastinator in your writing.

First, let us consider re-organizing the furniture in your home. Start in your living room. Is your living room couch where you want it? Is it a located in an inviting place? Would you like to sit there and relax when you take a break from your writing schedule? Can you picture yourself sitting there with a cup of coffee or tea in your hand? Chances are that the answer to this question is "no" because you have never looked at your couch with a writer's eyes before. Now go through your house room by room, looking with your new writer's eyes, and see what looks harmonious and what needs changing.

Does your home need painting? You may never have noticed the paint before. We can tell you from our experience that if your home needs painting, you will be thinking about this constantly while you are sitting at your desk trying to write. It is better to get it done now if it is necessary. You can easily do it yourself. Just buy a few gallons of paint and set aside a weekend or two. How much better you will feel when it is finished!

Of course, this may be a problem for your partner. He or she will not be seeing out of your eyes because he or she isn't thinking about writing. Therefore, disorder doesn't matter in the same way. In fact, your partner may not experience disorder in any form. This doesn't mean that it isn't there. Yours is a writer's orientation. So you must be patient and explain as carefully and lovingly as you can what it means to you to re-arrange the furniture in the living room, dining room and, most likely, the bedroom. The painting may seem even stranger to your partner since you never seemed to care before, but he or she will be happy enough when it is all over.

You may find that once you paint the areas that need painting, your curtains begin to look a bit dingy. Again, this is the kind of disharmony that will trouble you every time you sit down to write even though your curtains looked pretty good to you before. It's probably a good idea to go out and buy your new curtains now. But, before buying them, you might want to call in your local interior design person to help you with suggestions about window coverings. There are all kinds of new possibilities that have become popular since you last thought of window coverings (that is, if you ever thought about them at all). Ask for an estimate about how much these will cost. Once you have this estimate, you will probably decide to buy curtains at the local thrift shop or to sew them yourself. We guarantee that the combination of rearranging furniture, painting, and obtaining new window coverings will allow you to delay your writing for some appreciable amount of time.

It is not just the inside of the house that is important. The garden or patio is where you go to relax. It is where you go to reduce the stress of the writing process and so it must be a place of beauty and serenity. Have you ever worked in the garden before? Well, this is a good time to start. Doing your own gardening will give you a different feeling about your home. Then your writing, if you ever start it, will reflect the tranquillity of your physical environment.

If you don't have a garden, you can buy a large number of house plants. Fill the rooms of your apartment with plants and flowers, constantly changing them to get a sense of movement and growth. You can hang plants from the ceiling and the walls as well as placing them on tables or on the floor. The overall effect will be *like* a garden. A writer needs an environment that is alive and vibrant and that is just what you are providing for yourself.

Sidra Scrubbing the Kitchen Floor

This is Sidra scrubbing the floor of the kitchen. You can see the joy and satisfaction that lights her face as she cleanses the house in preparation for a writing session.

It is amazing to see what happens when you sit down to write a book. Everything imaginable that needs doing, might need doing, or could conceivably need doing far into the future comes to your attention. Isn't it better to take care of your home immediately, before you start writing, so that you can have a clear mind, free of these distractions once you begin to write? Any reasonable person would answer "yes" to this question. Many have followed our suggestions about rearranging their work spaces and have been very pleased. To appreciate the importance of these suggestions, just read this letter that we received from one of our satisfied readers:

> *Dear Hal and Sidra,*
> *I have been a professional woman and a writer all my adult life. My home never mattered to me. I just wrote books and articles and paid no attention to where I sat when I wrote them. Then I came upon the chapter on "Organizing Your*

Home" in your latest book and suddenly light bulbs started to go off in my head.

I looked around me and saw my home with new eyes. After all these years I have finally found within myself my "Inner Mother" and my "Happy Housekeeper". I had lost them both when I rejected my real mother at the age of three months. She was the total housewife/mother type and I never could bear being with her. I thought she was the ultimate bore.

Now, with the help of this wonderful book by you, Hal and Sidra Stone, I have given up writing and my life is filled with the richness of housekeeping and motherhood. I am now ecstatically pregnant and the doctor said it might be triplets. My 5 dogs and 8 cats make it difficult at times to maintain order, but for me it is a full time job. I feel as though I have finally "come home" to my real self and my true calling. Now all I need is a husband but I know that I will meet the right man soon.

Deidra Swallow
Awesome Wells, Arizona

Not all of our letters have this dramatic a conclusion. We are very happy to welcome Deidra to the world of non-writers and we certainly hope that she meets her husband-to-be very soon.

Hal Cleaning Out His Files

It is essential to have clean and ordered files for any kind of writing. Here we see Hal faithfully going through his files making sure that all is ready for his writing routine. Hal is an expert in cleaning out files, even the files that have been already re-organized.

9

Organizing Your Office or Work Place: Creating the Proper Mood

Believe us when we tell you that the advice we give is not merely theoretical. We have tried each of these methods and they have worked for us. They are guaranteed to work for you!

I f order in your home is important to your well-being as a writer, imagine the significance of the actual room in which you do your writing. It is essential to create an environment here that supports your writing and that stimulates the creative muse that is in you. The gods and goddesses of creativity simply cannot operate in a messy room. They need order to do their best job.

Let us start with your desk. You have probably owned it for a long time. Now, however, you have a new computer and an organized home. Do you want to write at the same desk or table that you have been using all these years? Wouldn't a six-foot desk be better than a five-foot desk? Mightn't it be better if your desk was deeper and had more file space? Are you satisfied with your bookcases? Now might really be the time to totally change your writing room to make it compatible with the new ambiance that you are trying to create. Perhaps some appropriate art for your walls? Maybe a new rug?

But we digress. Back to the desk. There are so many different desks to choose from! You can buy them in sectional pieces in black, in white, in designer colors, in wood, in glass and even in terra cotta. (Hal bought one in terra cotta a while back. It only took him a month to find it but this was a marvelous month of successful non-writing.) You can buy rolling file drawers and rolling storage units. You can even order special pull-out drawers or special computer tables for your new computer and printer. If your tastes are more traditional, you can buy a desk of pure oak. You won't be able to move an oak desk for cleaning once it is set up, but no one will be able to steal it and you don't really have to worry about cleaning underneath it for quite some time. If you do try to lift one of these it is important to realize that hernia surgery is quite simple and perfected these days and if you have good health insurance, it shouldn't be too expensive.

This is the perfect time, with or without new book cases and file drawers, to reorganize your books and files. The book you plan to write will require ongoing research so this additional organization will feel very good to you. Just imagine what it would be like to sit down at your new desk with all of these new things around you. Close your eyes for a moment and visualize all of your files and books in absolute order. Visualization is an excellent tool to help you see what you need to buy in order to continue this organizational process and support yourself as a writer.

While you are reorganizing your study you do have to remember to talk to your insurance agent and make sure that your new computer and printer and the furniture are all covered by your home insurance policy. This is very important and will help in a small way to delay the writing. As we say repeatedly, "Any delay is a good delay." By the way, are you satisfied with your current insurance? Is your coverage sufficient? Is your agent reliable? All this may seem silly to you, but we always come back to the same reality: writers need peace of mind.

We also strongly recommend a box of new pencils freshly sharpened with your new electric pencil sharpener. Even though you are writing with a computer and a word processing program, you still will be recording notes and making corrections. Besides the practical side of a sharpened pencil, there are the aesthetic considerations. Writers have been sharpening their pencils or taking care of their writing instruments for hundreds, even thousands, of years. You are a part of that tradition.

Since order will ultimately support your writing, you may want to consider purchasing an electronic organizer. Right now you are probably using a bulky calendar book to hold your appointments, phone numbers and "to do" lists. The electronic organizer allows you to record all of this information in just one very small piece of equipment that you can easily slip into a pocket or a handbag. By taking care of this small matter, you are left with a much simpler, more satisfying, and better organized life. It is true that it will take you several weeks to learn how to use this new organizer and to record all of your old phone numbers onto it. In the end, however, lies peace and order, a clear desk and a few more weeks of non-writing.

Believe us when we tell you that the advice we give is not merely theoretical. We have tried each of these methods and they have worked for us. They are guaranteed to work for you! Both of us are geniuses, each in our own way, at utilizing organizational principles for non-writing. We are currently considering a special training program in organizational non-development that will focus on the creative aspects of re-organizing your life. Please contact us if you are interested.

10

Organizing Your Finances

Now that you have become familiar with the more esoteric aspects of computer lore, you can begin to use a software program that allows you to computerize all of your personal and business financial affairs. This is a natural extension of your current organizational mode.

Your financial situation is no different from anything else in your life and environment that suddenly requires organization once you have decided to write a book. Happily, you are now the owner of a state-of-the-art computer. With this computer, an entirely new world is open to you, a world in which financial order reigns supreme. Once you have mastered the simple complexities of computerized bookkeeping, accounting, tax preparation, budgeting, stock reports, portfolio management, etc., you will know true peace of mind. You will be able to write your book with a mind clear of any kind of financial anxiety, clear of murkiness and clear of any troublesome thoughts about money.

Since we are currently concerned with financial matters, it would seem appropriate, at this point in our narrative, to sound a cautionary note about your finances. By the time you finish buying everything necessary for your home, your office, and your computer, it is quite possible that you will not have any remaining finances to organize.

Many of our recommendations **do** require serious expenditures of cash and some of our readers have gotten into financial difficulty because of this. We feel that it is important to bring this aspect of our advice to your attention. We want you to read the following letter because it gives a clear warning about some of the dangers of our recommendations:

Dear Dr. Stone and Dr. Stone,

I want to thank you very much for your recent book on non-writing. I have enjoyed it very much and it has helped me to put off my writing for a year now. I see no reason to believe that anything will change in the future. I have come up with one problem that I do want to share with you, however.

After I read your chapter on computers, I went out and bought two full sized computers, an IBM® and a Mac.® I just couldn't make up my mind as to which one to get. Then I felt I needed to have a portable system so I bought an IBM® compatible and a Macintosh® PowerBook. I know this sounds foolish, but, again, I couldn't decide which was best.

After this I bought an expensive color printer and all the equipment for interactive video. I joined Internet, AOL and CompuServe, even though I didn't need all of them. I have a new desk, new bookcases, new files. I even hired a part time secretary to help me to organize my files. I bought new furniture for my office and installed new carpeting. (You might want to come to visit me sometime to see all this. It's really beautiful!)

Besides all this, I fell in love with my new secretary and so I have gone into therapy to try to work things out with my wife who is very jealous. So far I have spent a total of $43,297.29 on equipment and furniture. My monthly bill for secretarial help and therapy is about $1,800.

*If you have any recommendations about all this, I would
very much appreciate hearing from you. I think I will be a
very successful non-writer for many years to come.*
                              Sincerely yours,
                              Bertucci Reynaldo
                              Port Everglades, Florida

"Forewarned is forearmed." Please do not follow our recommendations blindly. After all, financial organization is of little help if you have put yourself into serious debt. We are in ongoing contact with Bertucci and we have every reason to believe that things will work out to his ultimate benefit. In the meantime, he does have several used computers for sale should you be interested.

We trust that you have already become familiar with the more esoteric aspects of computer lore. Now you can begin to use a software program that allows you to computerize all of your personal and business financial affairs. This is a natural extension of your current organizational mode. The word "quicken" until now has been associated with going faster, or coming alive. Now it will have a very different meaning. Quicken® is a program that you can use to handle all of your financial records. It will no doubt take you several weeks to learn how to use it, but once you have learned it, everything financial can be entered into this system. Listen to the following letter that we received recently from Bjorn Rasmussen in Oslo, Norway:

*I was well on my way to writing a book on "Skiing in the
Nordic Countries" when I came across this book by the Stones.
I got very excited when I read the chapter on finances. I ran
out and bought a new computer and Quicken® but, unfortunately, I had no money of my own to enter into it. Undaunted, I began to enter in the money of all my friends. Now
I am a bookkeeper in Norway and I am very happy.*

I have hated skiing since I was a child. It always terrified me but I was ashamed to admit it before. This single chapter completely transformed my life. Thank you, thank you, Hal and Sidra for your deep wisdom and perceptions.

We wish to make clear to our readers that we are not anti-skiing. It is just that these are powerful ideas and once one is diverted from the writing track, amazing things are very likely to happen. Thank you, Bjorn, for your good wishes and sentiments!

11

Developing
a Writing Schedule

It is the Superman or Wonder Woman in us that creates these schedules but it is the ordinary human being who must carry them out.

I f you want to write a book, the worst thing that you can possibly do is to sit down and start writing! This causes nothing but confusion. (It is also possible that you actually might *write* the book and that is not what this book is about.) Instead of writing, what you must do first is develop a writing schedule. That way you will know when you will be writing, how long you will be writing, and how your writing is going to fit into your overall schedule of personal and professional activities. If by some strange twist of fate you find yourself writing and you do not yet have a schedule, you must stop immediately. It is never too late to develop a schedule!

Once you have your schedule, it is essential that you train yourself not to write at non-scheduled times. Keep in mind the need for a balanced life so that you do not end up without a relationship, without friends, in possession of a badly toned body, an unhappy dog, a bad relationship to your children, confused finances, and on and on. You do not want to let this happen to you!

Developing a writing schedule can be a great deal of fun. We are experts at this and have been most creative and prolific in the variety of writing schedules that we have developed over the years. Sometimes they have lasted as long as a week, which we consider a fairly long period of time. Hal considers himself to be particularly adept at scheduling and many a book and article has gone unwritten while he works on his schedules. He takes great pride in his accomplishments. His schedules are quite beautiful on their little colored cards or in his big agenda book. The computer, needless to say, adds an entirely new dimension to the creation of attractive schedules.

You can write out your schedule on paper or large index cards. Or you can begin to use your computer to outline different writing schedules. There are many different kinds of writing schedules you can follow. Our advice to you is to be creative and to try them all. Do not be afraid to experiment and to change your schedule.

One of the most exciting things about developing a writing schedule is that you can plan anything and do anything when you are creating a schedule. It is the Superman or Wonder Woman in us who creates these schedules but it is the ordinary human being who must carry them out. Because of this difference between who plans and who carries out the plans, we are required to create new schedules over and over again. Remember this: **the more schedules that you create, the less time you spend on actual writing!**

We have another rather brilliant recommendation for non-writing that we wish to share with you. Whenever you are creating a schedule, the ultimate purpose of which is to maintain your non-writing status, create the schedule **after** you have had two or three mugs of strong coffee. Two mugs of coffee is actually four cups and, after this much caffeine, you are ready to create a truly challenging schedule, a hyper-schedule, so to speak.

This "caffeinated scheduling" allows you to plan to get up at 3:00 AM. or 4:00 A.M. and exercise, meditate, do personal writing, go for a walk, feed the dogs, help with the children, find time to be with your partner, organize the various environments that you have created, and even have time to work on your book. If you are a morning person, this might work for a time, but if it was planned on coffee, you can be confident that the crash will come. When it does, and you discover that you cannot, in reality, handle your caffeine-induced schedule, you have to spend time creating another one. We refer to this as multiple scheduling and we are sure that it will bring you great pleasure.

Non-coffee planning can be just as effective if you are willing to go all out in your effort to create the proper schedule. If you feel that the topic you are writing about is special and if you see it as the basis for a special book, then you most certainly must create a special schedule that can do the job. You must take time, as much time as necessary, and try many schedules before you will arrive at the final one, the one that is truly special.

Don't throw away the different schedules you create in your search for the perfect one. You will find yourself coming back to them in later months and years as the effort to avoid writing becomes increasingly difficult. On the other hand, throwing old schedules away has its advantages because then you must re-create them from the beginning. Anyway, the real joy is in the creation of the schedule and not in the finished product. We are process-oriented people and feel very strongly that it is the process of not-writing that is important, not the finished product.

Though we strongly believe in the creation of your own schedules, we are preparing a 300 page manual on *The Tao of Writing Schedules* You may order this manual from us when it is finished. But first we must figure out our new schedule for completing it.

In the meantime, we would like to supply you with at least one sample schedule to give you some initial ideas. There is no single "right" way to do this. Be as creative as you wish in your own scheduling. The following is but one possible scenario in the life of a non-writer:

A Non-Writing Day

5:00 AM Alarm rings to start writing schedule.

5:00-5:15 AM Struggle to get up.

5:15-7:00 AM Back to sleep.

7:00-7:30 AM Shower and dress.

7:30-8:30 AM Exercise.

8:30-9:00 AM Light breakfast. Relationship time.

9:00-9:30 AM Meditate (This can also be done before exercise)

9:30-10:30 AM Record dreams. Do personal writing.

10:30-11:00 AM Coffee break. Play with pets.

11:00-Noon Make personal phone calls

Noon-1:00 PM Work on book outline

1:00-2:00 PM Lunch

2:00-3:00 PM Rest

3:00-5:00 PM Straighten office. Continue research on book and book series. Make fresh ground coffee. Feel bad about not having done more. Do some work with your Inner Critic. Possibly go for a short walk.

5:00-5:15 PM Stretch neck, back and wrists. Hang upside down.

5:15-6:30 PM Plug into information network. Send Email to appropriate people.

6:30-8:30 PM Dinner. Time with family and friends.

8:30-10:00 PM Movie for relaxation.

10:00 PM Critic Attack for watching movie.

10:15PM-12:01AM Work on new writing schedule. This one obviously won't do.

Sidra on StairMaster

Here is Sidra looking fit and trim, experiencing the dramatic impact of some of the ideas she will soon be communicating when she begins her writing session — once she is through with her dreams, personal writing, morning walk, feeding the cats and goldfish, having a leisurely breakfast and making sure that she has quality time with Hal. How ready she will be for writing when all is complete, except for straightening up the house of course.

12

Organizing an Exercise Schedule

Without endorphins and the feeling of vitality that comes from exercise, your mind goes dead and your writing is in danger of becoming dried up like an old prune. The only question is: "What kind of exercise routine do you want to follow?"

O ne of the worst things that you can possibly do to yourself is to start writing a book without being on a proper exercise schedule. We can hear your incredulous voices speaking to us right now, especially those of you who may not be on a regular exercise schedule. You are asking us: "What in God's name does exercise have to do with writing a book? I haven't worried about exercise up until now. Why should I worry about it now?"

The reason you have to start exercising now is that exercise helps your writing. It gives you a more balanced life and becomes a part of your regular, everyday routine. You can also involve your partner, and/or children, and/or dog in your exercise schedule. That way you get a double payback, you can exercise and relate to your significant others at the same time.

Writing is a very sedentary activity and the last thing in the world you want to do when trying to write a book is to sit still all the time. You need those endorphins flowing through your body to maximize your creativity! Without endorphins and the feeling of vitality that comes from exercise, your mind goes dead and your writing is in danger of becoming dried up like an old prune. The only question is: "What kind of exercise routine do you want to follow?" Needless to say, developing and implementing a proper routine can take a good deal of time that might otherwise be spent doing you-know-what, so please pay attention because this is an important chapter.

Your options for an exercise routine are as follows:

1. You can join a gym and spend a few hours a day in this way. As part of this option, you can hire a personal trainer who will help you to structure your program and, at the same time, let you know how much you need the exercise.

2. You can buy gym equipment for your home or office. You can buy a stationary bicycle, a weight machine and possibly a treadmill, a Nordic Track or a Stairmaster. If you add to these a few dumbbells and a machine that allows you to hang upside down, you are pretty well set up. You may well be laughing at the idea of buying a machine that allows you to hang upside down. However, after a few weeks of following the recommendations in this book and not writing, you may feel some stress which is quite likely to locate itself in your back. If you happen to have tried our methods and they haven't worked and you find yourself actually writing, hanging upside down will help you to stretch out and move the blood to your head. With this blood you get increased oxygen and, obviously, this will help your mind to function more effectively. Thus, in either situation, your new equipment will be useful.

3. Some people just run or walk near their home. This can be very relaxing but isn't quite as successful for non-

Hal Upside Down

A real writer must keep the Chi energy flowing. Hal does this in different ways. Here we see him hanging upside down, stretching his back and spine so the Chi energy can flow properly. If you hold this picture upside down you will notice the peaceful expression on his face. In this way Hal doesn't lose himself in the writing. Rather he loses himself in non-writing because he and Sidra have achieved mastery in this art.

writing because it takes less time and is very efficient. You can compensate for this efficiency, however, if you have a well-endowed Inner Pusher who doesn't let you stop at the proper time, but instead pushes you to walk farther each day.

4. No physical routine is complete without stretching. You can do this by starting Yoga, by working with a teacher who facilitates stretching or, if you must, you can just stretch. The latter has disadvantages because of the minimal amount of time it can take.

5. You can combine all the above options in which case you can be assured of a very healthy body. You can also be fairly well assured that no book will emerge from the depths of your new computer. If your computer gets lonesome, there are great computer games you can play with your family, partner, friends, and children.

Listen to the following letter that came to us recently from a reader in Utah:

Dear Hal and Sidra,

Thank you so much for the wonderfully clear insights that your book on non-writing brought to me. I have been a meditator most of my life. I was on the verge of writing a book that I had tentatively titled: Learning to Be or Not to Be.

The week I was about to start writing I came across your book and though many of the chapters were helpful to me, I found the chapter on exercise particularly brilliant. I started exercising immediately and I followed all the options you listed.

I cannot tell you what it has done for me. I have stopped meditating completely and now I have a job as the assistant manager of a health club just one block from my home. The girls there look really great in their cute little outfits!

I work out every morning in the gym; I stretch in the afternoon; I run in the late afternoon; I do a second aerobics at night on my new equipment at home and I swim on Sundays. Who has time to write? Who cares?

I admire your courage in speaking out on these matters. Thank you so much for finally making non-writing a legitimate activity! I no longer feel uncreative, unproductive, and ashamed. Thank you! Thank you! Thank you!

Jimbo Larrimer
Ocean View, Utah

Exercises

1. Close your eyes and visualize yourself doing twelve different things that require physical exertion. (Note: Sex

does not qualify as one of these activities.) Pay attention to how they feel. See which ones feel good to you and which ones feel bad to you. Jot down on a piece of paper which ones feel good to you for future reference.

2. Visit a store that sells home gym equipment. Try out the different equipment. Then visit two other similar stores and try the equipment there. As you try the different machines, again see which ones you enjoy and which ones you don't enjoy. It is the ones that you don't enjoy that you will probably buy because they are the best for you.

3. Visualize yourself at the age of 90. How do you see yourself? Are you unable to move around? Do you look old and decrepit? You are looking at the person you are to become unless you mend your ways. So get your schedule started and start to move that body today!

Sidra Thinking

The trick in non-writing is to plan and outline your material over and over again. Here we see Sidra considering her fourth book outline. Her serious intent is obvious to anyone who looks at her. You may be sure that she has mastered the organizational aspect of non-writing.

13

Organizing Your Book

As Hal's grandmother used to say:
    "Sloppy outlines make for sloppy writing."

Who could possibly write anything, especially a book, without outlining what it is you want to write about? Obviously it isn't possible, nor is it to your advantage if it were possible. If this were to happen, you literally might just sit down and write. Not so fast!

The purpose of the outline is to help you to structure your thinking. You don't want sloppy thinking, nor do you want to thoughtlessly express your personal feelings in a messy disorganized fashion. The more thorough the outline, the better the possibility for clear thinking and good writing. As Hal's grandmother used to say: "Sloppy outlines make for sloppy writing."

Books can go in many different directions and one of the advantages of outlining is that you can do more than one outline and thus permit yourself much greater freedom in determining the direction that your particular book will take. Multiple outlines give you multiple options so it is to your advantage to consider this possibility.

The computer is a wonderful instrument for creating outlines. There are all kinds of possibilities for indentations and markings. You can change fonts and font size. You can even add color if you have purchased a color computer and printer. You may think that you have enjoyed outlining in the past but, believe us, outlining with your new computer will be a very new and delicious experience for you.

There are deep outlines and shallow outlines. Needless to say, we are proponents of the deep outline. What this means is that you take the time to go into the sub-headings, then the sub-headings of the sub-headings, and then the sub-headings of those sub-headings. Your book is almost written for you by the time you have finished this type of outline. Listen to the following excerpt from a letter we received from Gulfsport, Wyoming. We think it illustrates the power of the outlining process and the kind of difference it can make in your life:

> *Dear Drs. Stone and Stone,*
>
> *I always pictured myself as a writer. After publishing nine novels, eight children's books and four volumes on the functioning of the thymus, adrenal and pituitary glands, this seemed a reasonable self-image. Then I came across your chapter on "outlining" in your recent book on non-writing. I was astounded!*
>
> *I suddenly realized that I have never enjoyed writing. I have been fooling myself for years. What I enjoy is outlining, deep outlining. So, my dear friends, I have become a professional outliner and if you decide to write another book and need delay, I can guarantee you a deep outline that will prepare the way for a blockbuster book.*
>
> *I am enjoying the outlining so much that I am currently planning to submit a book of outlines for publication.*
>
> > *Mitzilou Waring*
> > *Gulfsport, Wyoming*

We don't expect miracles all the time, but Mitzilou is quite typical of our respondents who take the time to work on these ideas and take them seriously. Thank you, Mitzilou.

Section III

Emergency Measures To Slow You Down If Our Initial Suggestions Have Not Stopped You From Beginning To Write

14

Complaining and Whining: The Compleat Guide

Most people consider whining, or whinging as the Australians say it, a terrible personality trait. We disagree. We believe that whinging can be a totally creative act when done consciously, with awareness, and in the service of non writing.

Distracting yourself from the task of writing by complaining or whining is not one of our most common approaches to non-writing. However, there are people who find this particular tactic very successful, so we thought that we should include it. The more we have worked with it, the more we realize that this can be a very successful technique. It all depends on your level of mastery.

Before we go any further in our explorations of complaining and whining, we would like to pay homage to the Australians who have a truly wonderful word for it! They call it "whinging." Doesn't that sound superb?

Now, on to the task of creative whinging! First, you must decide what you are going to complain about. Will you whine about the weather? your health? your relationship? your mother's treatment of you when you were a child? your father's lack of interest in your creative process and his insistence that you get a job? your lack of opportunities? your lack of training as a writer? the fact that the writing school you went to killed your creativity by teaching you how to write? the invasiveness of your family that interferes with your creative process? the necessity that you earn money when all that you really want to do is to write?

The list goes on and on. There are endless possibilities. They all add up to the feeling of "Poor me!" This is followed by the thought "I have had (am having, or will have) a more difficult life than you. There is so much I need to overcome, it's exhausting."

Now that you have decided upon the subject, or subjects, of your complaints, you must decide how to go about your complaining. Will you sit alone and brood or will you complain to others? Although we don't want to be considered sexist, we have found that sitting alone and brooding is particularly effective for males. Sitting alone and feeling sorry for yourself can immobilize you if you do it correctly. Just think of how much money you must earn to support your family before you will have the freedom to write! Think of how unappreciative everyone is. Think of how demanding everyone is; how much they all expect from you financially and emotionally; and how much time and attention they all want. Think of how nobody in your life has ever really understood you. The trick here is to think about all these things by yourself. Do not share your complaints with anyone who might be able to help you. After all, if they did help you, you would then be free to write.

Again at the risk of sounding sexist, we have found that women do best when they complain to another person, preferably to an understanding, motherly friend. Now there is another level of decision-making. Do you complain over the phone or do you complain in person? Is it better to whine over drinks or during dinner? Do you join a group and whine to the group or do you complain to one individual at a time? Or, do you do all the above? These decisions will affect the amount of energy and time that is devoted to whining and, consequently, spent away from your desk. This is all very valuable non-writing time because it absorbs a great deal of creative thinking and emotional energy that might otherwise be spent on your writing.

If you wish to expand from solely personal concerns, this is a good time to think about the deterioration in the quality of life. Think about the breakdown of institutions that have, in the past, been a support. Then there is always the government. That's good for a lot of complaining. The best whinging is when you collect all these individual complaints and then can feel sorry for yourself because you were not born at a different time in history. Or, perhaps you were born at a different time in history, but things are just not the way they used to be.

This more societally-oriented whining is best supported by research. There are numerous well-meaning magazines and radio stations that will give you the necessary information and support for this kind of complaining. Just listen to them, and you'll have material for months of thoroughly-validated complaining. All this research and all the passionate discussions that will grow out of this research take time away from writing. Since this is our goal, this is another golden opportunity to not write.

We know some people that have become so excited about complaining about national and international concerns, that they have written nothing in years. They are in much demand at dinner parties, however, because they can stir up simply marvelous discussions about what is wrong with the world today.

If you would like to perfect your whinging abilities, do the following:

1. Make a list of all the injustices that you suffered: (a) at the hands of your family of origin, (b) during your first marriage, (c) during your current marriage, (d) at the hands of your children, your boss, your employees, or anyone else who comes to mind.

2. Give 10 different endings to the following sentence:

   Poor me, I......

3. Choose among any of the following complaints that apply. Repeat them like mantras. If none of them are appropriate, make up your own. Do this morning and evening, looking into the mirror with a sad face. Soon you will find that you have a "poor me" feeling all the time and you no longer have any enthusiasm or energy for writing. The best part of it all is that it is not your fault!

I could be a great writer if only......

   I had the time.

   I were richer.

   I had less money to worry about.

   I had gone to school.

   I had not gone to school.

   I had another job (or profession, or business).

   I didn't have a family to worry about.

   I had a primary relationship.

   I had a different primary relationship.

   I lived alone.

Sidra in Hammock

It is essential not to become stressed out during the writing process. Here Sidra demonstrates her ability to "be" rather than to "do." The hammock is an essential part of the writing process.

15

Daydreaming

If you are a potential writer, your daydreams are going to develop a very special focus. It is to our advantage as promoters of non-writing to support these daydreams because they do keep you very busy and can take a great deal of time away from the writing process.

Most people think about daydreaming in a very negative light. There are two major reasons for this. First, daydreams are considered a waste of time. Secondly, the things that we daydream about are generally very private. If you were at a party it is certainly conceivable that you might share with someone the fact that you had a dream. Under certain circumstances, you might even share the content of the dream if you felt that he or she was the kind of person who appreciated hearing a dream.

Can you imagine, however, being at this same party and sharing your daydreams with people? It is highly unlikely. We often daydream about things that we feel quite self-conscious or even guilty about, so our daydreams are generally relegated to the closet. If you are a potential writer, your daydreams are going to develop a very special focus. It is to our advantage as promoters of non-writing to support these daydreams because they do keep you very busy and can take a great deal of time away from the writing process.

The following daydreams are fairly typical for the writer to be:

1. Number of Books Sold

    These daydreams are concerned with the fact that your new book is going to sell a very large number of copies. When we say a large number, we mean a large number! We are not talking about 10,000 or 20,000. We are talking about 100,000 minimum, minimum, minimum! Half a million books sounds better. A million books seems more than reasonable; it seems inevitable. Over the years, with good foreign marketing and an explosion of interest in your field around the world, it could go to five million over time.

    To promote this particular daydream we recommend closing your eyes and visualizing your book on a separate table in the bookstore nearest you. On this table you see your book piled three feet high, filling the table. There is a special counter person handing books out as people grab them for themselves and their friends. If you practice this exercise, you will have a great deal of fun. It will also occupy a great deal of time and support your ability to visualize which is a real benefit for your own personal growth process.

2. Money

    This book is going to make you rich. In this daydream your publisher offers you a $100,000 advance on your book and royalties that are 50% higher than any other writer gets. In addition, you receive your royalties once a month accompanied by a lovely summary of sales.

    This is a wonderful daydream and it can certainly occupy a good deal of space and time, so enjoy!

3. Foreign Sales

    Your book is in demand all over the world and has been published in thirty different languages. Your daydream about book sales is coming to fruition and, in addition to this, the financial remuneration is growing by leaps and bounds. Oh happy is the day when the writers get their pay! This is a grand fantasy. We suggest that you visualize the book cover as it might look published in different languages. If you know any foreign languages, visualize a number of possible translations of your title. This one is very exciting and it really works.

4. Publicity and Promotion

     This is the grand finale of your daydream adventures, the tour de force of the aspiring writer's fantasy life – Oprah Winfrey. The daydream is simple. You have received a call to be on the Oprah Winfrey show. Just you and no one else. Oprah interviews you alone and at the end of the show she holds up your book and says to the millions of people watching the show: "This is one of the best books that you will ever read! I CAN'T RECOMMEND IT HIGHLY ENOUGH TO YOU!" What can we say? Could anything be more grand?

To support this particular genre of daydream we recommend that you see yourself on a variety of different television shows, interviewed by a number of different hosts or hostesses. For this daydreaming exercise we recommend Sally Jesse Raphael, David Letterman, Jay Leno, Maury Povich and, of course, Oprah Winfrey. As part of the daydream exercise, remember to incorporate into the fantasy how your parents and friends treat you after you return from your filming in New York or LA. It would probably be very helpful if you spent some time watching the different hosts on television to study their techniques. Watching TV day and night to research all the possible shows would make your visualizations more creative and prepare you for more effective daydreaming.

We hope that we have demonstrated to you how creative daydreaming can be. It is particularly valuable for your development as an aspiring non-writer because you can daydream at any time of the day and night and thus interrupt the writing process at will. Listen to the following letter from Joey Herrington of Papua, New Hampshire:

Dear Drs. Stone:

Thank you so much for your wonderful book. I had started to write a book on the sexual habits of Shetland ponies when someone gave me your book to read. I was thunderstruck by your chapter on daydreaming and how it could be used creatively. I practiced the exercises diligently for a month. Not only didn't I write the book, but I ended up going to New York and getting a job as an assistant producer on the Howard Stern show and I have never been happier. My daydreams become my reality from one moment to the next and I get paid for them too!

Thank you so much for your trail blazing work!

Joey Herrington
Papua, New Hampshire

Hal Making Coffee

Preparing coffee and tea and then taking time to drink these delicious drinks with leisure and charm is an important part of the non-writing craft. Hal is a zealot when it comes to coffee preparation as you can clearly see from the intensity of passion that is in his face. Note too that he pours two packages of coffee at the same time in preparing the brew. Internationally recognized and acclaimed as a coffee mavin, Hal has trained many people in the art of coffee making and he has students all over the world. We might add that he considers himself the world's expert on the subject of how one can stop drinking coffee. He has set a world's record in this area.

16

The Creative Use
of Minor Addictions

*There is no better time to take a break than when
there is something that must be done.*

In our society, the term "addiction" has a very negative
connotation. It conjures up images of all kinds of terrible
behavior. There are, however, certain minor addictions that
can serve the cause of non-writing in a wonderful way. We wish
to deal with several of these because they represent such creative
ways of interrupting the writing process.

1. Smoking
    Taking a cigarette break is not quite as popular as it
    used to be. There was a time, not that long ago, when
    the cigarette break was a way of life in western culture.
    In fact, there was a time not long ago when it wasn't
    even necessary to take a break because the cigarette was
    a natural part of work and play.
    Smoking while you write would not serve you, the
    aspiring non-writer, as well as taking a cigarette break.
    After all, if you could simply sit at your desk and smoke
    while you wrote, it would barely slow you down at all.
    Of course, if you smoke a pipe, the standard choice of
    the male writer of a bygone age, smoking at your desk
    takes an appreciable amount of time. What with clean-

ing your pipe, packing it, lighting it and then lighting it again, both of your hands are busy a great deal of the time. This is an excellent support of non-writing.

Not only is it impossible for you to write anything down when you are using both hands in this way, but you are most likely to have your greatest inspirations as you relax and smoke your pipe. By the time you finish your puff and put down your pipe so that you can record your wonderful idea, you will most likely forget it. The next hour or so will be spent trying to retrieve it. Have you ever noticed that the best ideas you've ever had are the ones that you forgot?

If you smoke cigarettes, however, you can smoke and write at the same time. That is, if this is permitted in your work space. It is the case, however, that smoking has become so unpopular in recent years that you will probably be required to leave your desk and go somewhere else to smoke. Sometimes you just have to step outside your door to reach the closest smoking area, but there are cases in which writers have been known to travel a much longer distance, for instance down an elevator and outside the building before they are permitted to light up. The time may come when it may be necessary for you, the smoker, to drive to some central underground location 20 or 30 miles from your home in order to have your cigarette. This hasn't happened yet, but it could be coming. You could of course carry your portable computer with you when you leave for your cigarette break, but this seems to defeat the purpose of the break, and our purpose too.

For the moment we must be satisfied with the requirement that you go outside to smoke. This can easily take ten or fifteen minutes and if you smoke often enough, we have successfully eliminated two to three hours of your writing time per day. So we want you to feel good about your smoking. Don't focus on the guilt and judgment that comes your way. Focus on this book and the principles we are putting forth. Appreciate the deeper implications of what smoking accomplishes in the service of non-writing. Guilt will only cloud your mind. This is why it is so important to enjoy your smoking breaks and thus enjoy the writing, or non-writing process.

2. Coffee Breaks

Now let us talk about coffee and tea breaks, though they don't feel quite the same as cigarette breaks. Coffee charges the system with renewed energy. The caffeine hits your adrenal glands. Suddenly your brain cells are on fire and you are ready to go. Nonetheless, if you take frequent enough coffee and tea breaks during the day, they will occupy a very large block of time. If possible, take these breaks separately from your cigarette breaks, so that they can take up even more time. You can even take a break and drink herbal tea, though this isn't quite as sophisticated as drinking coffee.

Ideally it would be nice for you to own a machine that could make a lovely cappuccino or latte for you. Lacking this you might see where the nearest coffee house is and consider going there for your coffee break. The advantage of this is that it will take far more time than grabbing a quick cup of ready-made coffee from the automatic coffee maker nearest you. Also, you can order a tea latte at the coffee house in case you don't want coffee. You could even bring along your outline for the book or develop a new writing schedule while you are sipping your brew. Sitting in a coffee house and sipping something, anything, while you write looks and feels great.

Ostensibly, the coffee break is to give you a chance to relax and re-charge. There is always the danger that it will serve you in such a way, that it will promote your writing. We can only hope that this will be effectively overshadowed by the frequency and the length of the breaks that you take during the day.

If you do not go out for your beverage break, we recommend that you make your coffee fresh each time rather than using a coffee pot that makes eight cups that will last all day. It is even better if you grind your own beans. Then you have truly fresh coffee each time and you are creating a kind of writer's ritual. By the time you grind the beans, heat the water, make the coffee, find just the right mug for the day, pour your coffee and put in your cream and sugar, you have used up a substantial amount of time. Best of all, you haven't even begun to drink your coffee.

Don't take your coffee (or tea) to the desk because then you aren't really taking a break. The best thing is to sit outside and play with the cats, talk to your partner, listen to some music and express yourself as the Renaissance person that you are. Now, totally refreshed, you will be ready to go back to work and get some serious outlining done.

3. Snacks.

Eating snacks doesn't sound very dramatic in relationship to most of the non-writing methods with which we been dealing. On the other hand it shouldn't be underestimated. Snacks serve two functions. You must stop writing to eat and, if you eat enough, you get tired.

If you get tired you must nap and if you nap you aren't writing, so it's that simple.

There is always the possibility of a third function that snacks may serve. The truly sophisticated non-writer adds a Critic Attack after each snack. The Inner Critic's comments about the unnecessary calories and the possibly addictive quality of the behavior make a winning combination.

4. Naps

One doesn't ordinarily think of naps as being connected to addictive behavior. However, the reality is that anything can be used addictively and naps are no exception. So please don't fight your need for a nap. Tired people make mistakes and that is the last thing you want to do on a computer. Rest whenever you need to. Close your eyes – breathe deeply – rest into yourself. "Napiness" is next to Godliness so enjoy yourself and take the time you need away from the writing to help yourself to feel more rested. Just remember, there is no better time to take a break than when there is something that must be done.

We are aware of the fact that this chapter on addictions is not a very dramatic one. Yet the methods described here work very well and, if used properly, they are guaranteed to eliminate many hours of writing time daily. If you don't smoke or drink coffee or snack between meals, that is indeed unfortunate. If, however, you do not indulge in any of these activities, we have tried our best to present alternative ideas for your consideration. So read on.

Section IV

Utilizing Interpersonal Relationships As A Vehicle For Creative Procrastination

Hal and Sidra in Energetic Linkage

This is Sidra in a bliss state because of the time that she and Hal have taken to work on their relationship preparatory to starting to write

17

Helping Others: An Absolutely Foolproof Way to Procrastinate

Historically women have outdistanced men in the successful utilization of this technique. Their role of caring for others has interrupted all but the most determined writers. However, with the emergence of the "New Man," men are applying these principles with greater and greater success.

For centuries women have instinctively known how to delay their writing indefinitely by helping others. They are the trailblazers in this particular mode of procrastination. There is some question about whether this proclivity is genetic or hormonal, but so far as we know, this has not been adequately studied. Whatever the case, women are usually more successful in this arena than men. Although we realize that this last statement might be considered sexist, we sincerely hope that it is not too inflammatory and we beg you not to be offended. We are interested in the creation of an effective non-writer, not in gender differences.

Now, on to the topic at hand. People are always coming to you for help. Even if they don't come to you directly you, as a sensitive person, can often see ways in which they **might** need your help even if they are unable to ask for it. If you are a good person, you want to do things for others. If you are always available to help people, then you will naturally take time from your writing to do so. Your non-writing approach to life will be supported and, at the same time, you will be doing a good deed.

For instance, now that you have learned how to use the computer proficiently, friends will call you with computer problems. "My system has just crashed. What should I do?" Another one will tell you that her cursor is stuck and seems frozen. Another one will want to know why his Quicken® program didn't handle his last bank reconciliation properly. Once you become known as an available expert on computer lore, there is no end to the questions that will come your way and the time it will take to answer them. Each question provides an excellent "break" that can easily be far more effective than all the coffee, cigarettes, snacks and naps combined.

There are innumerable ways that you can help people. A friend may be moving to a different apartment. Helping such a person can be a real gift. Someone's car breaks down and she needs a ride to the garage. Your best friend calls. He is very unhappy at work and would like to talk with you about it. Your girlfriend is trying to decide whether or not to take the promotion she was offered. Your best friend is having relationship problems and needs some advice. Your mother needs you. Your children need you. The cats have to be taken to the veterinarian. Your son's pet python is having an identity crisis. Everyone needs you!

Who can say no to a child who phones and wants to talk to you? Who can say no to a child who feels insecure and needs comfort from you? Who can say no to a child who just wants to be with you and sit with you while you are writing. After all, you have their promise that they won't disturb you. Children come first; of that there is no doubt. So give them the time they need so that issues of guilt will not cloud your writing.

A very strange thing happens once you start to write. The moment you close the door to your work room, it appears that everyone suddenly requires something of you. We're not sure exactly what it is that happens. Where one would think the closed door is a hint that people should stay away, what happens with amazing frequency is that it ends up being an invitation for people to come in and ask you to do things for them.

Recently someone wrote to us about his own experience with closed doors. He and his wife hadn't had sexual relations in over six months. His wife seemed to have lost interest. On the day he started writing (before he read our book), his wife saw the closed door, entered his study, and successfully seduced him. Such is the mystery and allure of the closed door.

When you think about it, what happens here is quite clear. Closed doors make people feel insecure, so they become amazingly creative in finding ways to get the door open. Do you want to be the kind of person who isolates yourself from your family and/or friends? No! No! NO! The answer then is to be available; to give, give and give. If your book takes a while longer to write, so be it. You are a good human being.

If you believe in reincarnation, better yet. In this case you realize that you will have many opportunities in the future to write your book. Why be in such a rush. Life and death are simply doorways into each other. Besides which, imagine what the computers will be like in your next incarnation. If you don't believe in reincarnation, don't worry. There are plenty of other reasons to be relaxed.

If you feel yourself weakening and starting to become selfish to protect your writing time, then we recommend reading a biography of Mother Teresa to help you become more balanced.

By now it must be obvious why this chapter is so important. Being available to enough people is almost enough, by itself, to see that your book never gets written! It is the height of selfishness to put your writing first before your duties to your fellow human beings. People will see you as selfish whether or not they tell this to you directly. The real gift here is to learn how to use

all your relationships as proper vehicles for effective procrastination and, in so doing, to attain the status of a successful nonwriter.

Sidra Cooking

Good writing requires a healthy diet with tasty dishes. Here is Sidra preparing a meal while Hal is setting the table and emptying the dishwasher. It is important not to rush meals. Rushed meals are a great danger for many writers. In this photo you can see the care and thoughtfulness that Sidra is bringing to her choice of spices.

18

Continuing to Fulfill Your Social Obligations

Writing a book is a time consuming affair. You might well be seized by the creative muse, gobbled up by her so to speak, and disappear into oblivion. There is real danger in this. You might finish your book and discover that you no longer have any friends because you had so thoroughly neglected them during the writing process. In considering this entire issue, do spend some time thinking about the karmic consequences of this kind of interpersonal neglect.

In the last chapter we discussed the general principles of helping others, i.e., of being available to them in their time of need. Now we want to look at the general meaning of social obligations and see how adherence to a few fundamental rules of social behavior can help deter, or perhaps even totally obliterate, any serious writing tendencies.

Writing a book is a time consuming affair. You may well be seized by the creative muse, gobbled up by her so to speak, and disappear into oblivion. There is real danger in this. You might finish your book and discover that you no longer have any friends because you had so thoroughly neglected them during the writing process. In considering this entire issue, do spend some time thinking about the karmic consequences of this kind of interpersonal neglect.

What all this means on a practical level is that you need to maintain your system of social relationships. You must do whatever needs to be done to achieve this goal. Most likely, this will involve staying in touch with others by phone, mail, fax or eMail. It is very easy to neglect this and feel that it is of no importance when compared to the idea of writing a book. Such is not the case, however. After all, what is the ultimate meaning of the writing with all of its fame and fortune, its prestige and status, if you end up with nobody left to talk to except your publicity agent and the 500,000 books you have sold?

This maintenance of social contacts requires a kind of mothering function in the writer. One needs to call people and "tuck them in." This is akin to having children and putting them all to sleep in the evening so that you can finally do what you really want to do. The problem here is that you probably know a great many people so this "tucking-in" process can take a considerable amount of time. Sidra is an outstanding "tucker inner" and she offers three day workshops on the subject four times a year.

There is a very strong positive correlation between "tucking-in" tendencies and one's ultimate success in non-writing. For this reason we recommend that you practice the exercises we have listed at the end of this chapter. If you do not heed our advice, you just might get seduced by the glamorous image of a successful writer and limit your social engagements and interactions so that you can get your work done. But if you do so, you run the risk of finishing your book!

Last but not least, remember the age-old concern: "What will people think?". You certainly don't want people talking about **you** as "the big-time writer who doesn't have time for his or her friends anymore." You certainly do not want to be the kind of person who abandons old friends or uses the telephone answering machine as a way of avoiding people. Successful non-writing means being available. Let other people use their phone machines to dodge calls. You want to be the sort of person that people can count on! To become a genuine non-writer, you must live a normal, ordinary life and do everything that you are supposed to do to take care of peoples' needs.

Exercises

1. Make a list of everyone in your family whom you need to call. Add to this the names of any other relatives you haven't called during the past three months.

2. Using the same criteria, make a list of all the others, not in your family, you need to call or whom you haven't called during the past three months.

3. Compare these lists with your spouse (or partner), if you have one, to see if there is anyone that you have overlooked.

4. Make a list of the people to whom you owe a dinner invitation.

5. Over a three day period, phone everyone in your life who needs calling. Relax, enjoy yourself, and take plenty of time with each one. Promise them you'll call them again next week.

6. See how much better you feel now that you have spoken with everyone. You have accomplished two major objectives. (1) You have not written anything during this time, and (2) everyone you know is still talking to you.

Inner Child Work

Hal and Sidra are pioneers in the field of Inner Child work, particularly with reference to its importance both in human and human/animal relationships. Here we see them walk their talk as they allow their inner children to communicate with each other. In this way they remain vulnerable with each other and thus maintain a truly strong connection that can withstand the rigors of writing a book — if they ever are able to start it.

19

Enhancing Your Primary Relationship

It is imperative to review your primary relationship and discover what could be improved upon. Look for what is wrong and then fix it! Do not under any circumstance embark upon writing, which is a very significant undertaking, with a relationship that is anything less than ideal. It would be like setting out to cross the Atlantic Ocean in a leaky boat.

If you have followed our suggestions in the earlier chapters and have not yet become a non-writer, now is the time to take a moment and think about your primary relationship. You may well ask, and we would well understand your question and judgment, what on earth does your partnership have to do with writing a book or doing something of real significance? Please reserve your judgments until you have completed this chapter. By then, we are sure that you will feel as we do, "A good relationship is essential for proper writing."

Are you absolutely certain that things are going well for you and your partner? Do not be satisfied with a superficial consideration of your relationship. Even if everything looks just fine on the surface, is there anything you might possibly have overlooked? A relationship that is not functioning smoothly is going to create tension and anxiety and this will interfere with your ability to write. Therefore, it is imperative to review your primary relationship and discover what could be improved upon.

Look for what is wrong and then fix it. Do not under any circumstance embark upon this very significant undertaking with a relationship that is anything less than ideal. That would be like setting out to cross the Atlantic Ocean in a leaky boat. The following are some areas that might need attention:

1. Communication: Do you talk to each other? (Sometimes? Always? Never?) Do you share your feelings with each other? Your dreams? Your fantasies?

2. Do you have quality "quiet time" with one another?

3. Are you energetically connected?

4. Do you share common interests? Common activities?

5. Do you ever daydream about other possible partners? other living arrangements?

6. How is your sex life? Could it be improved upon?

7. Do you still get into bonding patterns, either positive or negative?

8. If you feel that your relationship is going well, might you be in denial?

We hope that these questions give you some guidelines with which you can evaluate the current state of your relationship. Once you have discovered the areas of difficulty, this might be a good time to go for couples' counseling or to attend workshops on how to improve your relationship.

Remember, there is no time like the present to clear up those remaining dysfunctional patterns from your childhood! Don't take a chance on having them trip you up now. Stop all bonding patterns before you move one step further. After all, you've cleaned up your house, your work space and your finances. Shouldn't you do the same for your relationship? Isn't it of equal importance? Dysfunctional relationships are obviously going to lead to dysfunctional writers. There is no point in becoming a successful writer if in the process your relationships remain dysfunctional.

Ask around for advice as to how you might do this best. Use this as a time to phone your friends (see Chapter 18) so that they will feel included in your process. Ask them if they have heard of any good couples' workshops. If they have any good ideas, run these by other friends, or maybe your therapist, to see what they think.

It is important to realize that writing a book is a real challenge for a primary relationship. Although your partner tells you that your time away is acceptable, even important, **you** know that this is simply not true. Beneath that self-sufficient, understanding exterior lurks an Inner Child who will feel abandoned the moment that the computer is turned on and you get involved in your writing. You must be aware that the Inner Child of your partner is going to have a love/hate relationship with your computer and your writing.

One way in which you can maintain the intimate connection that your partner's Inner Child wants is by "processing together". Processing together means sharing feelings with each other and reacting to one another. You will find that when you close the door of your room so that you can write, your partner (or his or her Inner Child) is likely to decide that this is a good time to process with you. Closed doors are an invitation to processing. From your partner's standpoint, not processing is equivalent to not loving and the last thing you want is to be accused of not loving.

Here is something else to worry about before you finish your book. Once your book is written, what will you say about your "significant other" in your dedication and acknowledgments? Will there be adequate recognition of the relationship's importance? When you become a celebrity and appear on all the talk shows, how do you think your partner will feel about all the time and attention that you are getting? Is this all worth the trouble? Yes, just think about that: "Is this worth the trouble?" If your answer to this question is "No", then you may stop writing at once and be done with it.

Sex is an issue that has to be attended to if you are to be a successful writer. Whether you are a man or a woman, you naturally will need your sex on a regular basis to stay relaxed so that you can approach your writing in a relaxed mood. Also, since you will probably be more cut off from your partner in a writing routine, sex can serve to connect you when you are disconnected. Of course, your partner may well object to this. Many people today have become quite fussy about a quality psychospiritual connection in approaching sex. This new attitude does make for problems for the aspiring writer.

Many women writers feel that they have an "obligation" to keep their partners happy and satisfied so that they (the writers, that is) can write in peace. This is one of the Inner Patriarch's basic rules. Some aspiring writers solve this by using sex as a kind of payback mechanism for all the deprivations suffered by the partner as a result of the writing. On the other hand, many women today rebel against this internal requirement and no longer feel they owe their partners anything in return for the deprivation they suffer. This, too, can cause problems.

All things considered, this might be the perfect time to take the Tantric sex class that you've always yearned for. Perhaps you could take it on Maui or in Bali and combine it with that romantic vacation alone that you've been promising yourselves. This way you could try to take care of the whole payback issue in one fell swoop. You might even enjoy it. Of course, when this is over, you'll have to go back to work for a while to fill up the bank accounts that have been depleted. This can be quite effective in helping to reach our long range goal of non-writing.

Sometimes this last move is the one that can delay your writing indefinitely as it did for the Duponts who wrote to us from Fiji:

Aloha Hal and Sidra!

We are practicing our Tantric sex, making shell jewelry and giving wind surfing lessons here in Fiji. A friend gave us your book and said that we should read it before we wrote our planned history of Aztec sexual mores. So we did.

We followed all your suggestions. First we set up our home and office environment so that we could devote our lives to our writing project. Then we bought new computers and organized all our finances. In organizing our finances, we made the amazing discovery that we had an extra $282,312.33 in an investment account that we didn't know existed. It was a gift given to us by Will's father over 20 years ago. What a boon and we feel we owe its existence to you at this point.

We were still considering writing our book when we read Chapter 19 and that was it! We decided to take a Tantric sex seminar on Maui. From there we traveled to Fiji and we have never returned home.

Since the computers don't work too well here on the beach, and we've lost our interest in civilization, we had to find an alternative way of earning money. If you ever come to Fiji, we would love to give each of you a complimentary wind surfing lesson at the new school we have established with our newly found money. We are calling it "Water Sports for Sports." We thank you for your vision and help!

> *Gratefully,*
> *Willy and Ariel Dupont*
> *Plantation Island, Fiji*

Hal With Cat

It is very important to not become too self-important in writing. Paying attention to your relationships and especially your pets is part of the humanizing process that we all need. Such kindly activity also keeps you from writing and thus two goals are fulfilled. Here we see Hal practicing this powerful non-writing method with Annie, one of Hal and Sidra's two cats.

20

Maintaining the Quality of Your Relationships with Your Children and/or Pets

Children tend to be more problematical than pets, although this is not always the case. A brisk walk and game of fetch does not always work for a child.

Now some might object to including children with pets, others might get miffed about including pets with children, but we feel that they can safely be grouped together when we talk about writing. Basically, neither children nor pets can be left unattended during the writing process.

This means that they must be thoroughly loved, fed, and exercised before you begin. Also, you must never lose touch with them while you are in the process of writing. This is usually the responsibility of the mother, but we know many fathers who take this aspect of writing quite seriously.

Pets are somewhat simpler to deal with than children. For instance, a good meal, a long brisk walk and a good game of fetch usually does quite well for a dog who is then likely to stretch out in a corner of the room and go to sleep while you work.

Cats, too, if you feed them something really expensive, pet them, assure them that they are the center of your universe and then provide them with a comfortable place in the sun are likely to nap. However, some cats enjoy the clicking sound of type-writers or computers and will want to walk across your key-board. It can become extremely difficult to maintain the much-desired cordial relationship as you try to remove your cat from your keyboard.

We had one cat who decided that she rather enjoyed napping on the keyboard. This was most unfortunate. Either we had a happy cat or we got work done, the choice was ours. Our sug-gestion, if you wish to become a non-writer, is to let the cat sleep on the keyboard until she is finished. This suggestion alone might move you into permanent non-writing status since your cat will most probably decide that your keyboard is hers and never allow you to use it again. Another possibility, as yet un-tried by anyone we know, is to buy a second inexpensive com-puter for your cat. The problem is that the cat will probably want to lie on top of the one you are using. Please send us your own experiences around this issue.

Children tend to be more problematical than pets, although this is not always the case. A brisk walk and game of fetch does not always work for a child. An outing with children, on the other hand, may take a full day or a weekend. A trip to the local theme park (Disneyland® or Disneyworld® would be prefer-able) can begin to make you, the devoted parent, feel that the upcoming involvement in your book has been partially paid off. A week of wilderness camping or a week in the local mall, depending upon your child's interests, can also help to balance the books.

We have found that at times when you really need to concen-trate, straightforward bribery can help. A promise of something really good, like a movie and a McDonald's® dinner, can often earn you several uninterrupted hours at the computer. How-ever, it is important to take each child's individual needs into consideration when arranging the bribes. This can require a fair

Sidra on Phone

Staying in touch with family and children and friends is a very important part of the non-writing process. No one wants to be accused of becoming too impersonal or driven by the need for power and success and money. Here is Sidra practicing her craft and deeply connecting to one of her children as her computer gets a well earned rest. Sidra has three daughters and one stepdaughter and one stepson besides a wide range of good friends. If she is true to her non-writing craft, she will be on the phone for a considerable period of time.

amount of time and sensitive negotiating skills, for instance, when one child wants to see *Conan the Barbarian* and the others want *Little Women*. Differences in food preferences must be considered here as well. Basically, bribery doesn't work unless you are able to give each child what he or she wants. Smaller, same sex families and or groups of children in multiplex movie theaters are a definite advantage here!

For the parent, or parents, who have access to child care, there is another set of considerations. As we noted in the title of this chapter, you don't want to lose the quality of your relationships. You don't want your children to forget you! Bad child care is unacceptable, but if the child care is really good, your children

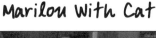

Marilou With Cat

Cats are essential to effective non-writing. They need to be played with and they also like to sit on the computer keyboard. Here is Marilou, our office manager, giving the cat the attention it deserves as she tries her best to work at the computer. She is trying valiantly to look as though she is working, but it is obvious that she is failing. After all, this is the idea, isn't it? Besides this, look at the beatific look on her face. These are the true rewards of learning the non-writing craft!

would have a wonderful time and just might cease to be unhappy about your unavailability. This can create a different kind of problem.

To guard against being forgotten, set the alarm on your computer (or if you are low-tech, set an alarm clock) so that it will go off periodically. When the alarm sounds, stop work and go to visit with the children in your home. Interrupt whatever they are doing, remind them of who you are, stay with them until you make meaningful contact, and then return to your writing. This is, most certainly, an effective way of slowing down your writing process. We cannot, however, guarantee what it will do for the relationship with your children.

If your children are grown, keep in touch with them regularly, perhaps daily, by phone or fax. If you are high-tech, send them eMail. Whatever you do, don't disappear from their view!

To summarize, if you want to stay related to your children and your pets: (1) give them whatever they want and (2) be sure that you pay them back for any time that you've taken for yourself. The term we have coined for this process is "balanced guilt." The following exercises should help you to work this out:

Exercises

1. Get a two column ledger. In one column, write down the hours that you have taken by yourself to write. In the other, keep track of the hours you have spent with your children or pets. Be sure that these are evenly balanced. If there is an imbalance, be sure that it is never in your favor.

2. What are your pets favorite activities? Favorite foods?

3. Plan outings for the entire duration of your book writing. This will require frequent discussions to make sure that everyone's needs are met. Then make the appropriate travel arrangements and reservations.

4. Buy a fax to keep in touch with older children. Buy them fax machines so that they can receive the faxes you send. Spend a few more weeks or months on income producing work (not writing) to pay for these fax machines.

Section V

Utilizing Personal Development To Interrupt The Writing Process

Hal Writing Down His Dreams

Here is Hal sitting at the patio table writing down and thinking about his dreams. Note the large pad he is using. This allows him to draw pictures that go with his dreams as well as making notes on the morning stock reports as they come in.

21

Dreamwork as a Method for Avoiding Writing

If you can spend an hour or two on your dreams each morning, this is an hour or two that you will not spend on your writing. Since the early morning hours are particularly significant for most productive writers, this will guarantee that each day starts out as a non-writing day.

Nowadays, it is vital that we each pay strict attention to our own personal growth or transformational process. Our society is in a turmoil and we each must do what we can to right the imbalances that lie behind its disturbances. There are many ways we can do this, but certainly one of the most significant is to work on our own personal processes in an ongoing manner, no matter what else we may be doing, and this includes writing.

If you are writing a book that deals in any way with the problems of society, it may seem paradoxical that we ask you to put your personal process first. Isn't it reasonable, however, to make sure that your own head is on straight before you start to try to straighten out the thinking of the rest of the world?

There are many ways in which to work on one's own transformational process and the simplest place to start is by recording one's dreams every morning. Dreams show us how we are out of balance. They are constantly attempting to compensate for the way we are thinking, feeling and behaving in life. They do this by bringing up the opposite side, by trying to show us what is missing from the way we are perceiving and experiencing the world.

Of particular importance to you as an aspiring writer is the fact that the dream process is connected to your creativity. Your dreams bring you messages from other dimensions of consciousness and they open you to new possibilities and feelings. In doing so, they open you to the entire creative process in its ever changing forms. The trick, then, is to record your dreams every morning.

Before you begin, you must find the right book in which to record these dreams. Take your time, do some serious comparison shopping. Although you might decide to write your dreams in your computer for easier access and legibility, a beautiful dream book is a joy forever. Many bookstores and better stationary stores have magnificent collections of journals and dream books for your consideration. This is a good time to allow your inner shopper to enjoy herself or himself thoroughly. This part of the process could well take days.

If you don't remember your dreams, then we would recommend that you spend some time reading one of the many excellent dream books that are available. This will help to stimulate your unconscious. You might want to read a variety of dream books anyway. Not only will they help to stimulate your dreams, they will tell you how to remember them. They will also give you excellent suggestions as to how you might record your dreams. We also suggest that you buy a number of books on dream interpretation so that you will have some ideas about how to interpret the dreams that you will be writing down. Actually, you might want to listen to our dream tapes at this point in your process, so that you can hear our ideas about dreams. In addition to reading books or listening to tapes, there are always dream groups that will give you the chance to share your dreams with other people of similar interests to your own. You may even wish to consider the possibility of seeing a therapist who specializes in dream work as a way of learning more about the subject.

Writing your dreams every morning is just a part of the story. You must also write down your associations to the dreams and then try to figure out why the dream is coming at this time. What is the message? What is it trying to say to you? **What is the relationship between the dream and the book that you are trying to write?** One of the easiest things that you can do with a dream is to close your eyes and re-visualize the dream. Go through it again and pay attention to what you see and feel. If someone else is present to share this with, this can be helpful as well. This kind of sharing can also help you to maintain the intimacy in your close personal relationships that were discussed in the previous section of this book.

We hope that we have made clear that the dream process is very important, that it can give you valuable insights into your own psychology, and that it can help to deepen your creative process. What we have not mentioned, is that it is exciting and fun to work with your dreams and that it takes a great deal of time. We know some people that have become so involved in their dream work that they have abandoned their writing completely and become successful non-writers. They spend hours and hours each day writing their dreams, associating to them, interpreting them and cataloguing them. Some more high-tech ones have even joined on-line dream groups in cyberspace.

It is important to note that the dream work is generally done early in the morning upon awakening. If you can spend an hour or two on your dreams each morning, this is an hour or two that you will not spend on your writing. Since the early morning hours are usually the most productive time for writing, this will guarantee that each day starts out as a non-writing day. Actually, any additional rituals that you can build into your early morning hours is money in the bank so far as non-writing is concerned.

We hope that this brief overview of the dream process is helpful to you and please believe us when we tell you that if you begin to take your personal growth work seriously, there is no end to its power to deter your writing. We are including this letter from Anna to give you a sense of how successful this method can be. Please understand that in publishing these letters we do not in any way or at any level wish to toot our own horns. We believe deeply in our ideas and we feel that these letters might help you to clarify your own process.

> *Dear Hal and Sidra,*
>
> *I so much appreciate the gift that you have given to all of us. My father was a famous Tasmanian psychiatrist and I was immersed in psychology all my life. My father hated dreams, however. He said that they were the tools of the Tasmanian devil so I never paid any attention to them. I have written a dozen books in the field of personal growth and I had just started a new series of 4 books having to do with male/female relationships in the Australian Outback when I came across your book.*
>
> *Your chapter on dreams rocked me as nothing I have ever read before. I began to record my dreams, associate to my dreams, visualize my dreams, paint my dreams, make clay figures of my dreams, meditate on my dreams, and share my dreams with friends. I am so excited by this wonderful new world that I am trying to read every book that has ever been written on dreams.*
>
> *I realize now that my father was addicted to writing, just as I have been. He hated dreams because they represented non-writing and, until recently, I had been following in his foot-*

steps. I am so grateful to you for your work and for helping to free me to become the non-writer that I was meant to be.
Anna Floyd
Tasmania, Australia

Truly, a dream in time saves nine!

22

Meditating as a Way to Delay Writing Each Morning

If there is a chance that meditation will deepen the creative process, then it certainly behooves you to take it very seriously because anything that deepens the creative process is going to be good for you.

Meditation has become increasingly popular over the past 30 years as a vehicle for personal transformation and spiritual growth. Unfortunately, not everyone enjoys practicing meditation. If this is the case with you, you may substitute additional physical exercise in the morning or additional time with your partner, children, pets and dreams. Fortunately for all of us, there are a vast multitude of ways to avoid writing each morning if we only have the vision and courage to discover them.

Back to meditation. The simplest form of meditation is breathing. Breathe in and count to four as you do so. Make your breathing very slow. As you get to the top of the breath, pause for a moment and allow yourself to feel that moment of fullness and then release the air, again to the count of four and as slowly as you can. When you get to the bottom of the breath again pause for a moment and feel the emptiness there before you begin to inhale again.

Anyone who meditates has to deal with the issue of distraction. The mind brings the most amazing things to us whenever we try to be still. In order to deal with the activity of the mind, one can use a mantra as a way of staying focused. A mantra is a word or an expression or a sound that you repeat to yourself, silently or out loud, to help you to maintain your focus. The mantra will generally have some special spiritual meaning and there are many mantras to choose from. The mantra can be tied to the breathing exercise we described above and this makes for a very effective basic meditational technique.

Meditation allows you to become quiet and centered when it works. This being the case, it will have an effect on your creative process. If there is a chance that it will deepen the creative process, then it certainly behooves you to take meditation very seriously because anything that deepens the creative process is going to be good for you. If meditation doesn't work for you, then your Inner Critic has one more thing to criticize you about (see Chapter 27).

There are many meditational techniques and this is not the place to describe them all to you. There are many books on the subject and no end of people who would be only too happy to tell you how to meditate. From our perspective of non-writing, the important thing is to develop the habit of meditating for at least an hour every morning and, if possible, every afternoon.

If your morning routine includes meditation, dream work, Yoga, aerobics and some personal writing (see Chapter 23), you have gone a long way towards meeting the goals of this book. Add to this some quality time with your partner, children (if any), and the morning news on radio and/or TV, and your morning will certainly be complete. If you follow all our suggestions, by now you should have arranged for sufficient activities to keep you busy through mid-morning. This is splendid, because soon it will be lunch time and you will then have a natural interruption built into your writing day.

Anything that you do or use in life can be used creatively either as a support or a hindrance. This is particularly true for meditation which might very well **help** you with your writing rather than slow it down. Non-writing requires daring, courage, imagination and a willingness to take risks. If you are not vigilant, your meditation might well help you and, before you knew it, your book could be moving towards its final phase. We recently received a letter from Sunshine Scrimshaw who told us of his "near-writing" experience.

Dear Hal and Sidra,

I feel that I must share my near-writing experience with you so that it will be of assistance to others on the path of non-writing. I had started to write my third book, Overspending by Swiss Peasants, *when I first discovered your remarkable book. I began to follow your program carefully, chapter by chapter.*

Each chapter was a new revelation, but it was the meditation chapter that really helped me the most. At first my meditations helped me to focus upon my work. I was more relaxed, I wrote more easily and my writing style became elegantly simple. I knew that I had made an error. I was destined to become a non-writer and here I was writing more beautifully than ever! I knew that I was having a near-writing experience, something I wished to avoid. I returned to the book and I reread your chapter on meditation. Finally I understood what you meant! Meditation was meant to delay *my writing, not to* improve *it.*

I have now followed your advice properly and, through my meditative practice, I have discovered the ultimate delay. I have become a devoted devotee, living in a Swiss-owned Ashram in Southern India. I meditate most of the time and, in addition to the fact that I no longer write books about subjects that don't interest me, I don't have to live in those miserable freezing mountains any longer.

Sunshine Scrimshaw
Formerly of Switzerland
Currently Living in Southern India

23

Personal Writing

Personal writing can be more effective than anything we have discussed in this book if it is approached with the proper attitude because you can write and write and write and never become a published writer.

P ersonal writing is an important part of our morning program of personal growth and transformation. It is a natural accompaniment to dream work and meditation. We would recommend that it follow these. Most individuals first meditate, then record their dreams and then do personal writing. Each of us has a different rhythm, however, and you can schedule these activities in any order that you wish.

You have no idea how much you are going to enjoy your personal writing! You may have been focused on your book, but personal writing opens you to another world, a new dimension of living. Not only that, but you will enjoy the excitement of doing your personal writing on your new computer and experimenting with the differing effects of the various fonts.

The basic principle of this chapter is to realize that personal writing opens up the "writing pores". You are writing directly from your feelings and experience. There is no audience. You are not writing to please anyone. This writing is not going to lead you to radio and TV interviews. It is not going to get you anywhere except into the expression of exactly who you are, what you are feeling and thinking, and how you wish to express yourself as a human being. Personal writing means expressing your feelings and thoughts without censorship. Do you see now why the personal writing is so important and why it is that we need to keep the personal writing very separate from the book you are thinking about writing?

There is something else that you can do with this kind of writing. You can write directly to the figures in your dreams in a dialogue format. As a matter of fact, you don't have to limit yourself to dream figures. You can write to any of the many selves that live inside you. Not only can you write to them, but you can have them write you.

A number of experts suggest that you can write with your non-dominant hand in this process and thus allow the parts of you that are less developed to have a chance to express themselves. This can be a problem if you are using a computer. One possibility might be to use the computer with your left hand only and see if you can get the same effect. We haven't tried this ourselves yet but if this doesn't work, you can abandon the computer and shop for a beautiful journal in which to do your non-dominant hand writing. The search for the perfect book for your non-dominant hand could take quite some time.

You can do personal writing at any time of the day or night and this is very advantageous so far as your non-writing needs are concerned. We realize that this sounds confusing. However, it is important to prioritize your goals and be clear about where you are heading. Imagine that you wake up in the middle of the night with an inspiration for your book. This could be a very dangerous time! If, however, you are alert and wish to avoid one of those "near-writing" experiences, you could choose to do some personal writing **before** you start to work on your book so that you can be properly attuned when you start your book writing.

Thus, instead of writing your book, you could spend several wonderful hours writing personally, going over your dreams, writing to your different selves, writing out some of your visual meditations and allowing your fantasies to express themselves into your computer. Then, when you are finally exhausted, you go to bed a happy man or woman, supremely conscious, and still a non-writer.

We cannot recommend personal writing highly enough to you. On the computer, it is a joyous event, full of experimentation and high-tech creativity. In a journal, writing or drawing with your own hand, there is more a sense of intimacy. Journals, themselves, can be beautiful works of art with magical overtones. Do whichever suits you, depending upon your mood at any given time. Whatever works, works! That is our philosophy. Personal writing can be more effective than anything we have discussed in this book if it is approached with the proper attitude because you can write and write and write and never become a published writer.

24

Enhancing Creativity

The more that you do creatively, the more you will feel creative. The more that you do to feel creative, the less time you will be working on your book.

We have been dealing with the issue of creativity in the last three chapters of Section 5. These were the chapters on dreams, meditation and personal writing which are all invaluable in the creative process. However, since creativity is so important for the writer, we felt it was necessary to honor this subject with a chapter of its own. After all, being in touch with creativity is basic to the writer.

Anything that you can do to stimulate the creative process in you, other than writing a book of course, is very much to your advantage in both the preparation for, and the actual writing of, your book. What we would like to do in this chapter is to help you find activities that can stimulate your creativity and help you to see yourself as a truly creative person. It is very important that you have a clear picture of yourself as a creative being because this helps your writing to flow effortlessly. Now let us segue to specific suggestions.

Anything that allows you to tap into yourself more deeply is going to enhance your creativity. There are a number of very simple activities which can be surprisingly helpful. For example, many people will do some kind of painting, drawing or sketching. It isn't necessary to think about such work in a true artistic sense. It is a question more of learning to play with colors and forms as a child might play with colors and forms. It is necessary when you do this kind of expressive work to separate yourself from your thoughts so that you are free to let go and allow underlying feelings, colors and symbols to emerge in a natural way.

Working with clay will also encourage the emergence of your creativity. Take small pieces of clay and put them on a board and keep putting new pieces on top of the original ones; eventually something begins to emerge from the blob of clay. It may not be anything recognizable, but being recognizable isn't what you're after. You are learning to play with clay and allow it to develop in its own natural style. Creativity has to do with letting go of control, allowing yourself to be spontaneous for short periods of time. To develop this skill, you cannot be focused on results.

Another way to develop your creativity in relationship to your book is to write poetry. This is very stimulating because it gives you a way of expressing feelings that prose does not provide. You can start with very short verses. It is important not to worry about rhyming or elegance. What we are after here is a spirit of play and fun when you do the verses.

You can do any of these things on your own. However, it is also possible to take a class in writing or poetry or painting or sculpting or ceramics. As a student of non-writing, the important thing is to spend as much time as you possibly can developing and deepening your creativity. The more that you do creatively, the more you will feel creative. The more that you do to feel creative, the less time you will be working on your book.

To give you an example of how this works, listen to the following letter that illustrates the power of the creative process.

Dear Hal and Sidra,

Since reading your book, my life has changed completely. I have been a writer for 73 years. I started writing when I was 21 years of age and I have written over 178 books, 92 journal articles, 33 monographs and 98 mystery stories. Many of these were written under a variety of pseudonyms. I have won the Pulitzer prize three times and the Nobel prize for scientific research on four separate occasions. People think of me as un-usually prolific.

Nevertheless, when I read Section 5 of your book on per-sonal development, especially the last chapter on the develop-ment of creativity, it gave me a whole new outlook on writing and on life in general. I wish I had read your book when I was 55 years younger. I would have had a very different life.

To make a long story short, now whenever I sit down to write a book, article or short story, I realize that the work on my creative process is more important. Therefore, instead of trying to continue to write the book, I do dream work and meditation. I write poetry. I paint and sculpt. I have taken up ball-room dancing, Greek and country-western dancing as well as rock, tap and Yugoslavian line dancing. I cannot tell you how happy I am. My publishers are not so happy, how-ever, and you may be hearing from their attorney. I'm really sorry about that. I tried telling them about the theory behind non-writing, but they seemed entirely unappreciative of what you are teaching. They just want me to keep producing and doing, doing, and more doing! Thank you for restoring me to my Greek soul!

Thank you again for your work on behalf of my fellow writers and myself. I haven't seen my chiropractor in the seven months since I started this new regime. She is also not too happy with you, but I don't think she will sue.

Keep up the good work!

> *Samantha Jeffers, PhD,*
> *MD, MA, BS*
> *Club Med "GO" Staff*
> *Currently Cancun, Mexico*

We can well understand the problems that Samantha's publishing company and chiropractor are having with her new-found life. It is tragic that in their need for financial survival they cannot appreciate the new insights and the newly acquired creativity that is developing in Samantha. It has been true throughout the ages that there have been people who could neither understand nor appreciate the real meaning of the creative process and its significance for the evolution of civilization. We generously forgive them!

Section VI

Effective Distractions: Enlarging The Writing Task To Delay Its Completion

25

Writing Articles
to Prepare for
Writing Your Book

This particular distraction can create a very long delay, but only if it is approached properly. You can spend years writing articles and trying to get them published and never, ever get to your book.

At this point in the game, we have a right to be worried. If you, as a prospective author, are still reading this book, we must assume that you have managed to start writing your book. Therefore, we must shift our tactics. We will attempt to change your current writing program, the one that is allowing you to work on your book.

Our recommendation is that you consider writing some shorter articles before you continue with your book. Articles are valuable for a number of reasons. They are short and so you get immediate gratification for the work. You can submit them to magazines and journals and, if they are accepted, this, too, gives you a sense of immediate gratification. If you write a number of short articles, this will give you the sense of being a prolific writer, something that is good for your self image. Best of all, you will not get any work done on your book during the time you are writing articles.

Writing articles and submitting them can be a truly time-consuming task, particularly if you follow the steps we will now suggest:

1. Go to your local newsstand or supermarket to look for magazines. If they do not have a large selection, look elsewhere. Ask around, be sure to let your friends know that you are looking for magazines in preparation for writing articles. This is an excellent move since it will give you a chance to review Chapters 1 and 18 which cover talking about your work and keeping up your contact with friends. If all else fails and you cannot find the proper magazines, go to the largest airport near you. Large airports always have a broad selection of magazines.

2. Look at the popular magazines and periodicals. See what people are reading these days. Check out the writing styles. You might want to spend several days thumbing through magazines to see which would be most appropriate for your work. This is a good time to ask yourself: "For whom am I writing this book?" (Please note the proper use of the word "whom". As a writer, you have become very sensitive to the use of proper grammatical construction. You may well find yourself editing people's speech as they talk to you. This can be very embarrassing because you will find it difficult to pay attention to **what** they are saying. You will be too busy editing it.)

3. Buy the magazines that seem most appropriate and take them home with you. Read at least five articles in each. Now you know what style is required for each magazine and you can write your articles appropriately.

4. If your topic is a professional one, repeat the above three steps with all professional journals. Obviously, a differ-

ent tone will be required for the professional writing and you must always keep your audience in mind.

Trying to write for a variety of groups can be very confusing. This adds to the success of this particular distraction. We have found that some aspiring writers totally lose their sense of self and forget their own "writing voices" as they try to tailor their writing to the requirements of others.

This particular distraction can create a very long delay if it is approached properly. You can spend years writing articles and then trying to get them published. You might even look for a separate agent to act as your representative in these matters. Writing articles for magazines and marketing them is quite different from writing and selling a book.

As you spend weeks on this activity and you find that you want to get back to your book, tell yourself the following: "I can work on a book for a very long period of time without any idea of how it is going to be received by others. A few short articles will let me know if I am on the right track. Then I am in a position of making course corrections earlier in the process. I no longer have to wait until my entire book is finished. This will actually save me time and trouble in the long run."

If you are writing a book that is more scientific or professional and you are making progress with your work, then you might want to shift for a time and write a few short stories. This would give you a different kind of experience, make you feel that you are a "real" writer, and, at the same time, delay the completion of the book that you are writing. The trick here is to look at the kind of writing that you are **not** doing and consider doing some of that. Have you considered a screenplay? A novel? That might be fun to do.

Writing short articles on unrelated subjects gives you a chance to make use of your daydreams and really go hog-wild. Books can get very boring and you certainly don't want to be bored or become boring to anyone else. Can you even conceive of the number of different things that you are capable of writing about? There is no end to them.

As a result of following Suggestion Number 1 above, Todd and Maggie Hunter moved into a totally new field. They gave up their dreams of writing books and became paparazzi. They are now jet-setting around the globe, chasing celebrities and finding wonderful gossip to report in the magazines they discovered at the checkout counter of their local supermarket. As a sideline, and under a pseudonym, they write tasteful esoteric pornography based upon their daydreams.

We don't want to belabor our point here. If the idea of writing articles feels attractive to you and if it can distract you for a period of time, then all is well. If this does not work, then we suggest that you move on to the next chapter for more delaying tactics.

Hal Doing Research

Research is one of the primo methods for developing non-writing ability. Here is Hal engaged in serious research on his not yet started book. He is going to make sure that he has all the material at his finger tips so that no one will criticize him once the book is out. It is clear from this picture that Hal is a very serious researcher.

26

Research, Research, and then More Research

People don't criticize you for doing research. They do criticize you for the book you have written. So it is safer to do research. After all, you never know when someone is going to find some area of your writing that is based on inaccurate information.

Research is one of the main keys to a successful book. To research a book thoroughly is to know everything there is to know about the subject or subjects that are central to the book. This is as true of a novel – whether it is a romance novel, a mystery story, a piece of science fiction, or a historical novel – as it is of a doctoral dissertation or scientific research paper. Research grounds your writing so that whatever you portray is constructed upon a complex and realistic foundation. Research is a magic word in the writing industry and it is one of the most important tools that we have in the promotion of non-writing. So please pay close attention to this chapter because it could well save you from being overcome by your writing tendencies.

Usually we save our personal letters for the end of a chapter. In this case, however, we want to include a letter we received from a young graduate student on the East Coast. Her letter presents the case for research much better than we possibly could do ourselves.

Dear Drs. Stone and Stone:

As a graduate student I have done exceptionally good work. I was moving along the academic track and well on my way to my PhD when I came across your book. I found it just in time since I had already started to write my dissertation. I thought I was ready to write since I had already spent three years of full-time work surveying the literature and reading everything that I could possibly find on my topic: "An Examination of the Emotional Bonding Patterns of Men and Women and Their Computers." I had used libraries and computer information banks in this extensive research. My dissertation committee was pleased with my efforts and had given me the go-ahead. I even had a signed contract for a book based on my thesis to be published by Phantom House.

As you can see, everything was set and I thought I was ready to write. That is, I thought so until I read your chapter on research not just as a preparation for writing, but research as a way of life, a way of meeting the world that can be enormously satisfying.

Inspired by your book, I realized that research is a never-ending task. There is always new information. There are always new articles. I have added memory to my new computer that I bought after reading your book and I now have a storage space of ten thousand gigibytes. This means that I could store information for the next hundred years, including the Encyclopedia Brittanica, a hundred times over. That is exactly what I intend doing.

I thank you both so much for helping me to escape, by a very close margin, the possibility of finishing graduate school and becoming a writer. My parents are not very happy with my plans but I am talking to them regularly and I am sure that they will come around once they are finished paying for my new desktop computer, printer, portable computer and all the extras that go with them. I gave them a copy of your book and they promised me that they would read it. I do so much need them to understand me.

Sincerely yours,
Ernestine Masochisto
The Masochisto Research Institute
New York, New York

Ernestine has captured the essence of this chapter. The essence of writing is research. **It is the process and not the result that counts!** People don't criticize you for doing research. They tend to criticize you for writing books. So it is safer to do research. After all, you never know when someone is going to find some area of your writing that is based on inaccurate information. If your research is not complete, people can tell you that you are too subjective, that your writing is based too much on your feelings and not enough on facts, or that you are inaccurate in your description of things.

On the other hand, when someone asks you what you are doing and you tell them that you are doing research, they are very impressed by what they hear. When you are doing research, you can never be wrong. There is nothing to criticize. Critics do not criticize research, that is, unless you make the mistake of publishing it. Then you might possibly be in trouble.

Research is many-faceted as a support for the non-writer in all of us. In the beginning, research is an excellent preventative measure. If you get lost in your research, you can successfully avoid starting your book. Further along in your writing process, your research can delay you or even, if you follow our philosophy and the example of Ernestine, it can completely stop you from finishing your book. So keep Ernestine in mind the next time you sit down to write. At all costs, avoid just writing and having a good time. A serious commitment to research will change all that. With enough research nothing is fun anymore and your feeling of being a non-creative, non-writer may well be maintained, even if you finally **do** publish your book.

Section VII

Building
Low Self Esteem:
Two Sure-fire
Techniques For
Destroying Your Faith
In Your Work And
Your Ability To Write

27

Supporting Your Own Inner Critic and Perfectionist

The perfectionistic reworking of a single portion of your book is a foolproof method for interfering with your creative flow. Writing is no longer pleasurable, you feel as though you are working in the salt mines, in an airless chamber many feet below sea level. Everything you write with the help of your Perfectionist is a tiresome effort.

This is an extremely important chapter and may well save your life as a non-writer! We cannot emphasize this strongly enough!

I f your goal is not to write a book, pay close attention to this chapter. There is nothing like the deadly duo of Inner Critic and Perfectionist to keep you from writing. So, follow our advice here, and your ultimate success as a non-writer is assured. Or, at the very least, you should be able to slow down your writing process so that your book won't be finished before the beginning of the next millennium.

The basic question to keep in mind when you are trying to empower your Inner Critic and your Perfectionist is: "What will people think?" Picture others reading your book. For the

best results, picture the people in your life who are really important to you. What will they think of it? What might they say?
More specifically, what kinds of negative things might they say?
This sets the stage for the appearance of your Inner Critic and
your Perfectionist. Now on to the details!

The first step in the process of supporting your Inner Critic
is to invite him (or her) to the party. This is quite simple. Begin
at the beginning. When you wake up in the morning, have your
Inner Critic check over your dreams and comment upon them.
Do they give any indication that this will be a bad writing day?
Have your Inner Critic interpret your dreams in its own inimi-
table fashion, that is to say, in the most negative way possible.
Now worry about your dreams. How might they have been more
propitious? What did you do yesterday to make them so negative? Next take some time to worry about how much you are
going to accomplish today. Don't forget to worry about whether
what you actually do write today will be good. Let your Critic
help you with these worries.

The next step in this procedure is to create the necessary
ambiance. Your Inner Critic must be comfortable. This means
that *you* should be uncomfortable. Be sure that when you write,
you sit in a hunched over, anxious position at your desk. Try
hard, furrow your brow and keep your breathing shallow. If
possible, sit in an uncomfortable position with poor lighting. If
coffee makes your heart race, drink it. If you are useless until
you have had your first cup of coffee or eaten breakfast, skip the
coffee and the breakfast. Remember that anything you do to
make yourself physically uncomfortable and anxious will support your Inner Critic!

Now that you are seated at your desk, open up yesterday's
work and **let your Inner Critic review it! Don't forget to invite
your Perfectionist to join this evaluation!** This initial review
period is the best way to be sure that your Critic and Perfectionist will be present for the entire writing session. Once they have

entered, you will be happy to know that it is almost impossible to move them out. This is a good way to induce the famous malady called "writer's block", which sometimes proves terminal for writers, successfully and permanently turning them into non-writers.

The dynamic duo of Critic and Perfectionist will look over what you've written and they'll be happy let you know what is wrong with everything you've done until now. A major revision is obviously in order and revisions are good. The more the better. Everything will come out much better under the watchful eyes of the Critic and Perfectionist who are both revision specialists.

This is a good time to review alternative careers. Take a moment to relax, breathe deeply, and, when you feel relaxed and in touch with your deeper self, visualize all alternatives to writing. This exercise can take the remainder of your writing day.

Now that you have pictured alternative careers, and perhaps have become enthusiastic about one of them, you might want to call around to find out the requirements of the schools that you would need to attend. Ask them to send you brochures describing their programs. If you feel truly ambitious, ask them to send you an application for admission. Figure out where you are going to get the money to pay for the schooling that will be necessary before you will be ready for your new career. We unconditionally guarantee that all this activity will slow down your writing. If not, we will gladly refund the money you paid for this book.

Now that you have thought about an alternative career, let your Critic tell you what a wimp you are for giving up so easily. If your Inner Critic is a good one, you will be unable to write another word at this point and you should feel like a complete failure as a writer. If so, congratulations! Your self-esteem has been shattered successfully and you have joined the happy ranks of the non-writers of the world!

Inner Critics and Perfectionists love to make you feel that

you aren't yet ready to do something. This is one of the reasons why these two characters are so popular with psychotherapists. They single handedly support the psychotherapy profession by making people feel terrible about themselves. They make sure we feel that we are not ready for whatever it is that we want to do. In this way, they fully and unconditionally support our non-writing goals.

In the writing process, here is a good maxim to follow: Keep your Perfectionist around. This way, each paragraph must look perfect before you can move to the next. Be persistent. If a particular idea or image is not working out, do not discard it because, if you do, you might be sorry later. Just keep working at it. Let your Perfectionist take over your writing and try to figure out a way to make the idea or image work. The Perfectionist has incredible stamina and will never, ever give up. There's always a way to do "it," whatever "it" is. You can spend entire days fruitlessly trying to salvage a piece of writing in this way.

This perfectionistic reworking of a single portion of your book is a foolproof method for interfering with your creative flow. Writing is no longer pleasurable, you feel as though you are working in the salt mines, in an airless chamber many feet below sea level. Everything you write with the help of your Perfectionist is a tiresome effort. You can spend hours or even days trying to please your Perfectionist. In the end, whatever you write this way is usually pretty dry and boring. Needless to say, it is always the piece of work that your Perfectionist wrote that your editor cuts out of the final book.

With your Perfectionist helping you write, everything takes a bit longer. We recently heard from a man whose Perfectionist had taken over the writing of his book many years before. He wrote to us: "Thanks for your support and encouragement. Since I read your book, I now understand a great deal more about my Perfectionist. He has been helping me write about aging gracefully. We've already been working on this project for quite some time, but I just know that I will be finished in this lifetime. He assures me that if I listen to him I will be truly proud of my work." And we thank you, Methuselah, for your enthusiasm. Good luck to you. We look forward to seeing your perfect book that will one day be written – maybe.

As you can see, the combination of Inner Critic and Perfectionist is most powerful. We are happy to recommend them as writing companions in the adventure of not writing a book. If you insist on pushing through and writing anyway, we guarantee that they will slow you down to a snail's pace and, most assuredly, make the experience a most miserable one.

28

Seeking
Outer Judges

People love to judge others, and, with the right kind of encouragement, your friends, families and colleagues will find that they have a great many ideas about how you could improve your book.

Preparing yourself for the criticism of others is an important part of becoming a writer. You certainly want to be prepared for the absolute worst that can come your way. Therefore, find out what the masters in the field of criticism say. As any serious writer will tell you, listening to and reading criticism of your writing builds character. You can do this in a number of ways.

The first is research. Read book reviews in your field, as many as you can find. The more critical they are, the better. As you read the reviews, think of what your colleagues might say to you. Then ask them! Work with the people who are close at hand. Talk about your ideas and invite your friends and colleagues to comment upon them. Later, when you have begun to write, show them your work as it is produced. If they give a non-specific nod of approval, encourage them to think seriously about what you're planning to write and to be critical. After all, you want to discover possible weaknesses and correct them before you let the book move out into the world.

Be brave about this, because we all know that the ability to take criticism is a test of your strength of character. After your colleagues tell you what is wrong, ask them what you might do to make things better. Collect their suggestions. If they don't have many, ask for more. People love to judge others, and with the right kind of encouragement, your friends, families and colleagues will find that they have a great many ideas about how you could improve your book. Now think about how to incorporate all these suggestions into your work.

Don't settle for just one side of the story. If your work is controversial, ask for criticism from both sides. Everyone must be satisfied before you are truly finished. The more suggestions and criticisms that you can accumulate, the more work you will have to do before you will feel comfortable about giving your writing to a publisher. The more criticism you hear, the worse you will feel. But this is preparation for the reviews to come after your book is out there. Remind yourself: "If you can't take the heat, you'd better get out of the kitchen."

Sometimes there is so much criticism and so much to be done to improve your book, that you feel it is just too much trouble and you decide to write about something else. If this happens, and you do decide to abandon your current project and to begin all over with an entirely new subject, then start all over at the beginning of this book and follow our suggestions for your new book.

Once you have collected the criticisms of colleagues, move out into the general reading public. What might intelligent, well-read people outside of your particular field of interest have to say about your book? There are many places where you could see how your book might be received, but one of the best is the New Yorker. This is a publication that is famous for its brilliant put-downs. Only a magazine writer from England could possibly surpass the deft, death-dealing blows that you can find in its pages.

Once you have researched in this fashion, you are ready for the next step, which is fantasy. Imagine what people will say when they read the sentence you are writing at this very moment. If you do this correctly, sentence by sentence, the passions of your creative muse will be dampened significantly, they may even be totally squelched.

If you are blessed with a critical family, show your work to your family members and ask them for their opinions. They will probably be delighted to let you know what is wrong with what you have written. If they're really good at literary criticism, they'll be able to judge your basic ideas, the way in which you've developed them, your style of writing, your grammar, your spelling and last but not least, the typos that have somehow sneaked past your repeated proof-reading.

Exercises

1. Make a list of the five most critical people you know. Send them your work asking for their critique. Arrange luncheon dates with them individually, allowing plenty of time for discussion of your manuscript. Meet each of them and listen carefully to everything they have to say. Carry a package of Pepto Bismol® with you because you will need it.

2. Send your manuscript to your parents, particularly if they show little interest in what you do. Ask them what they think of it.

3. Read the *New Yorker* commentaries and visualize what they might say about your work. How might they make you look foolish?

4. Read as many British book reviews as you can. Make a scrapbook of the most cutting comments you can find. Read these each night at bedtime. There is a rather

famous Cole Porter song called *There's No Business Like Show Business*. Well, when it comes to criticism and judgment, **there is no judgment like British judgment** and we urge you to take full advantage of this major body of work.

Section VIII

If All Else Fails!

29

You Can Always Change Your Mind

I f you have come this far in reading this book and you are still committed to writing your own book, it is clear that you are stubbornly attached to writing and very focused in your approach to your work.

There is, however, one remaining possibility that we wish to present to you. This is effective at any stage of writing. You can use this approach when you are in the planning stage before you actually start writing, after you have begun to write, or when you are almost finished. It is even more effective if we have succeeded in helping you to delay your writing with the other suggestions we have earlier in this book. For example, if six months have passed since the time you first had the idea of writing a book and if you still haven't started it, or you have just barely started it, then our next recommendation could be valuable to you.

Think about your book. Do you still feel that your general outline would really interest people? Doesn't it seem that your original idea for a book feels somewhat flat at this point? When you first started the idea had a great deal of vim and vigor. Now, however, after all this time has passed, does it seem a bit drab and dull? It might even feel flawed, fatally flawed. Mightn't it be better if you thought of another topic, another theme, another title? Possibly, if you are patient, a dream might come that would bring you something that has a greater freshness and originality.

You mustn't feel depressed or defeated at the idea of giving up your original idea and waiting till a new one emerges. We probably just saved you an enormous amount of time and energy. Imagine writing a whole book and then realizing that the whole theme was flat, or that it wasn't really something that you wanted to do. Now, although you don't have your new idea yet, you are free to do personal work and to develop and deepen your creativity so that the new book topic has a chance to emerge organically from within, reflecting your deepest truth.

Changing your mind about what it is that you want to write is a time-honored and most legitimate method for deferring the completion of a book. It is better that you think of it as a "deferring process" rather than as "changing your mind again." The latter has more of a pejorative feeling to it and we wish to reassure you that deferring the beginning and /or completion of your book can really be viewed as a creative act that is ultimately in the service of your newly won status as a non-writer.

One of our readers sent us the following poems to describe her feelings about the non-completion of her book and about her own personal "near-writing" experience:

> *It was close, too close,*
> *I almost finished the book!*
> *How terrible that would have been!*
> *It really was so boring and so thin.*
>
> *It's lucky I read your book*
> *and chose to wait*
> *for something new and fresh*
> *for something alive and bold.*
>
> *Nothing old for me!*
> *I want a new and creative adventure.*
> *So what if I wrote 1800 pages!*
> *Does it matter? No!*
>
> *Yes, it was close, too close,*
> *I had almost finished the book!*

How terrible that would have been!
It really would have been a sin
to publish something
    so boring and so thin
        and so lacking in vim!
But the next one will be different!
             Mildred Rimmele

Mildred didn't fail in giving up the 1,800 pages of writing she had done. No, she was true to herself and to our principles. Clearly she is nurturing her creative process, waiting for the new flow from within! And as she waits, she is constantly reminded of how close she came to a "near-publishing" experience, one that might have been even more devastating that the "near-writing" experiences we have discussed. The next book will always be better. Why take a chance on this one?

Section IX

If You Must Write!

30

If You Must Write, You Must Write!

If at first you don't succeed as a non-writer, try, try again.

I f you have arrived at this chapter, we have failed you in your attempt to join the family of non-writers who are a part of our non-writing community. We apologize! The writer in you is clearly too powerful at this time and you are clearly too committed to the task at hand.

Please remember, however, that you can use these principles in your next book. Never assume that because you are well on your way to completing one book that you can't utilize the principles of creative procrastination in the next one. You are always welcome into our loosely woven organization and if you respect our ideas, we consider you one of us. This means that if you tried to follow our ideas, we consider you a part of our far-flung family of friends. We require no certification, membership pledges, or yearly fees.

For ourselves, we are thinking about a new book. Actually, we are each thinking about a series of books. This makes two series of books. We are starting to tell people about them and we would love to share our ideas with you. We also have a dozen or more outlines on file and we must sort through these as well as the thousands of dreams people have sent to us before our actual work begins.

We have joined an information network and this is going to take us many, many hours to figure out. Our personal work takes us a great deal of time and, as we get older, the considerations of soul-related issues become increasingly important. Our mornings are pretty well shot with all of our personal work, our exercise and taking care of our cats. We live our ideas, or "walk our talk" as they say and we are optimistic about the continuation of our non-writing capabilities.

Thus we are entering into the conflict phase of the non-writing process and the war has begun between the writer and the non-writer in each of us. We are planning to re-read this book every morning as a method of supporting our non-writers. If you don't hear from us again, we have been successful. If you do hear from us again – well, life could be worse! Please keep us in your prayers and send us any new ideas that you might have.

Hal and Sidra Stone
Albion, California
Begun December, 1995,
completion successfully delayed
until February, 1997

Appendix A

Bibliography

Hal Stone, PhD and Sidra Stone, PhD
You Don't Have to Write a Book
Delos, Inc. 1997

To our knowledge this is the first book written on this subject since the beginning of this century and we venture to say that we believe no one has seriously approached it since the beginning of recorded history. If you have titles that would be appropriate to this bibliography, please send them to us in care of Delos, Inc., P.O. Box 604, Albion, California, 95410-0604.

Appendix B

Unwritten Books by Drs. Hal And Sidra Stone

The following listing of book titles comprises a partial list of books that were planned but not written by the authors. We hope that this will be an inspiration to our readers. You will note that none of our proposed titles or topics has "Embracing" in it. After writing three books in our *Embracing* series even our most far-out fantasies do not include *Embracing*. In fact, so strongly do we feel about this that we even have considered a book on how to avoid *Embracing* in book titles. We rejected this as too ludicrous and have thus not even included it in the list below.

1. *The Dream Master* – Sidra and Hal

2. *The Psychology of the Transference* – Sidra and Hal

3. *How to Stop Drinking Coffee* – Hal (Hal is **THE WORLD'S** foremost expert on the subject of stopping coffee drinking. In fact, he has done it so many times that he is considering writing a book on the *Addiction to Stopping Coffee Drinking*).

4. *Workbooks on Voice Dialogue* – Hal and Sidra

5. *Workbooks on Relationship* – Hal and Sidra

6. *For my Daughters* – Sidra

7. *Don't Buy Your Daughter a Horse Unless You Are Filthy Rich! A Training Manual for Good Father Types* – Hal

8. *The Dragon's Teeth* – Hal

9. *A New Voice Dialogue Manual* – Hal and Sidra

10. Revise *Embracing Heaven and Earth* – Hal

11. Make a small book out of each of the audio tapes, with accompanying workbook – Hal and Sidra

12. *The Aware Ego: A New Vision of Consciousness* – Hal and Sidra

13. *Wisdom from My Grandmother* – Hal

14. *Luncheon Menus from Training Intensives at Thera* – Hal

15. Childrens book series on the *Psychology of Selves* – Hal and Sidra

16. *The New Spirituality* – Hal and Sidra

17. *Tales of Relationship: "The Snow Queen" and "East of the Sun, West of the Moon"* - Sidra

Appendix C

Written Books, Audio Tapes and Video Tapes by Drs. Hal And Sidra Stone

OK! We are not perfect. Here is a list of titles of works we slipped up on and actually completed. Forgive us.

BOOKS

The Shadow King, Sidra Stone, PhD
Embracing Heaven and Earth, Hal Stone, PhD
Embracing Our Selves, Drs. Hal & Sidra Stone
Embracing Each Other, Drs. Hal & Sidra Stone
Embracing Your Inner Critic, Drs. Hal & Sidra Stone

TAPES

Meeting Your Selves
The Dance of the Selves in Relationship
Understanding Your Relationships
The Child Within
The Voice of Responsibility
Meet the Pusher
Meet Your Inner Critic
Meet Your inner Critic II

The Patriarch Within
Children and Marriage
Affairs & Attractions
Our Lost Instinctual Heritage
The Pleaser
The Rational Mind
Accessing the Spiritual Dimension
The Psychological Knower
Indroducing Voice Dialogue
Voice Dialogue Demonstrations
Decoding Your Dreams
Exploring the Dark Side in Dreams
Reflections at 65
On Aging
Integrating the Daemonic
Visions & Prophecies

TAPE SETS

Voice Dialogue, Relationship & the Psychology of Selves
Making Relationships Work for You
Making Your Dreams Work for You
The Aware Ego

VIDEO TAPES

The Total Self
The Inner Critic in Action
Ending the Tyranny of the Inner Patriarch